THE YEAR OF THE TURTLE

THE YEAR OF THE TURTLE

A Natural History

Written and Illustrated by
David M. Carroll

CAMDEN
•HOUSE•
PUBLISHING

Camden House Publishing, Inc.
A division of Telemedia Communications (USA) Inc.

Library of Congress Cataloging-in-Publication Data

Carroll, David M.
    The year of the turtle : a natural history / written and illustrated by David M. Carroll.
       p.   cm.
    Includes bibliographical references and index.
    ISBN 0-944475-11-6   ISBN 0-944475-12-4 (pbk.)
    1. Turtles--Northeastern States. 2. Natural history--Northeastern States.   I. Title.
    QL666.C5C37 1991
    597.92--dc20   90-20388
                                                    CIP

Cover and inside color printed by
New England Book Components
Hingham, Massachusetts

Text printed and books bound in Canada by
D.W. Friesen & Sons
Altona, Manitoba

Edited by Jill Mason
Designed by Eugenie Delaney
**Camden House
Publishing, Inc.**
Ferry Road
Charlotte, Vermont 05445
First Edition

Trade distribution by
Firefly Books Ltd.
250 Sparks Avenue
Willowdale, Ontario
Canada M2H 2S4

ACKNOWLEDGMENTS

One does not get to devote countless hours to drawing and writing and to wandering swamps and marshes without considerable tolerance and assistance. Help and inspiration have come from many people over many years. I am indebted to their encouragement and grateful for the margins I have been granted.

I would like to acknowledge some of those who have been of particular help in the matter of this book. I am very grateful to Fred Courser and his family for the pleasure of freely wandering

Leatherleaf, *Chamaedaphne calyculata.*

the wetlands of their beautiful farmland. Similarly, I thank the Bates family. Jointly, these people have provided me access to extraordinary turtle areas.

Annie Burke assisted me greatly in aspects of turtle evolution, morphology, and embryology. Throughout her research, she has never failed to keep her eye on the marsh, and she has been an insightful and *simpática* co-wanderer of the turtles' world. Gordon Ultsch, with whom I shared boyhood searches for spotted turtles, has been an invaluable resource, particularly in regard to the ecology and physiology of hibernating turtles. I was fortunate also to be able to consult Terry Graham on turtle matters; he and Brian Butler shared field observations with me, especially concerning Blanding's turtles. Michael Klemens also contributed beneficial comments and insights. Carl H. Ernst provided helpful advice and information, and his extensive field work (particularly with spotted turtles) has been a reference treasure. Anyone with an appre-

ciation for turtles must acknowledge the leadership, inspiration, and efforts of the late Archie Carr.

I appreciate the long-term faith that my agent, Meredith Bernstein, has kept in assorted aspects of my work. Editorial Director Sandy Taylor has maintained a vision that has been central to the realization of this book. Jill Mason's sensitivity and expertise made the final editing phases more pleasure than work. Eugenie Delaney's masterful designing has given the art and text a beautiful form.

My wife Laurette has been a touchstone throughout this project, as she has been in the life and art that led up to it.

I have a deep appreciation for the many researchers whose devoted and thorough work has added to the knowledge of these remarkable creatures, the turtles. Any errors in the technical content of this book are my own responsibility.

I wish to thank anyone who has ever helped a turtle to cross a road, or worked to keep a wetland wild and free.

For Sibley

Rattlesnake manna grass, *Glyceria canadensis*.

CONTENTS

Foreword 8

Introduction 11

Chapter One: EMERGENCE 12

Chapter Two: COURTSHIP & MATING 42

Chapter Three: NESTING 62

Chapter Four: SUMMER 98

Chapter Five: HATCHING 126

Chapter Six: HIBERNATION 148

Captions for Color Plates 163

Selected Bibliography 164

Index 167

About the Author 173

FOREWORD

Viewed from atop a nearby ridge, an asphalt ribbon snaked across the valley floor. Early in the spring, it had replaced a winding dirt road that served this small rural community for over three centuries. Gargantuan sugar maples had lined this New England lane, their scarred trunks serving as silent warnings to those foolhardy enough to drive hastily. Heated opposition to paving this road had come from many quarters. Despite acrimonious town meetings, advocates of "safety" and "progress" had won out. The venerable maples were felled, and the road straightened, graded, widened, and blacktopped.

Descending from the ridge, I walked along the road, the acrid smell of fresh tar filling my nostrils. I was heartened to see that the gentle panorama of woods, fields, and scattered farmsteads appeared unchanged. A rapidly intensifying drone caught my ear; as I stepped back, a red Porsche whizzed by. The asters and goldenrods lining the road's edge bowed in the passing tailwind.

Rounding a wide curve, the road dipped to a small bridge, which crossed over a heavily shaded brook. Lying on the road's shoulder, partially obscured by the dappled sunlight, some all-too-familiar debris caught my eye. I gathered up the dried, shattered fragments of turtle shell and wondered if earlier this year the same red sportscar had cut short this turtle's life. The sharp-edged shell fragments poked through my pocket, jabbing at my thigh as I walked back up the ridge.

I have worked in museums for well over a decade, gaining an appreciation for the volume of information that can be gleaned from just a few pieces of a turtle's shell. Carefully removing these fragments from my pocket, I wondered what I was about to learn concerning this turtle's life and death. The first fragment was from the top shell, known as the carapace. Its distinctive blotched pattern of yellow on a dark brown background readily identified it as coming from an eastern box turtle. The next piece was the rear portion of the lower shell, called the plastron. It was flat, indicating that the turtle was a female. I was able to count the growth marks, known as annuli, on the plastron, and although they numbered twenty-four, some were beginning to wear off. Therefore, this turtle was probably between thirty and forty years old, not old at all for an eastern box turtle, which can live a century or more. I had also found some curled-up, Styrofoam-like material scattered amongst the bony turtle-shell fragments. These were dried-up eggshells. Like many of her kind, this turtle was killed while moving out of her small home range to search for a dry, sunny nesting site. The eggshell fragments placed the date of her demise in June, probably within the first two weeks of the month. The next fragment was a piece of carapace with a strange, marbled texture characteristic of scarred, regenerated shell tissue, usually resulting from a fast-moving brush fire. Another piece, from the periphery of the turtle's shell, exhibited well-healed tooth punctures and gnaw marks. In her three to four decades of life, this turtle's shell protected her against fire and predators, and would have easily done so for another forty years. Herein lies a much larger story of why the survival of over one hundred of the world's two hundred fifty turtle species is now in jeopardy.

———————⁓———————

For nearly two hundred million years, turtles have flourished on our planet. Many turtles became extinct long before the dominance of *Homo sapiens*, but the combination of protective armor coupled with a long reproductive life enabled turtles to survive into modern times. Although a small percentage of turtle eggs hatch, and an even smaller number survive to adulthood, once mature, turtles continue to reproduce for decades. Therefore, the individual adult turtle is very important to the survival of its species.

The primary causes of worldwide turtle declines are loss, fragmentation, and alteration of habi-

tat, as well as the ever-increasing removal of adult turtles from the wild. Examples of habitat loss range from the filling of small, wet meadows in New England to whole-scale destruction of huge tracts of Amazonian rain forest. Habitat fragmentation also is a global phenomenon and some serious examples occur in the northeastern United States. In southern New England, despite the illusion of an extensive forest cover, roads and development have fragmented habitats, bringing several species to the brink of local extinction. Habitat alteration is caused by a myriad of factors all over the world, including lumbering, hydroelectric projects, and pollution. For example, dams have been linked to the decline of turtles that require fast-flowing riverine habitat.

Other factors also reduce the number of adult turtles. Turtles are an important food resource in many parts of the globe. Burgeoning human populations, coupled with more sophisticated hunting techniques, have resulted in many turtle populations being overhunted. The wild-animal trade, whether in live animals for pets or in products made from turtles,

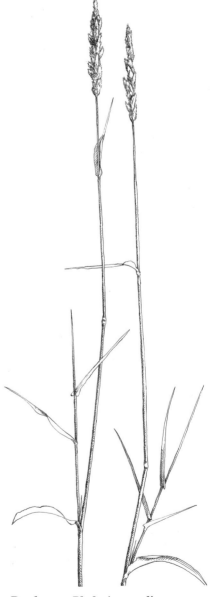

Reedgrass, *Phalaris arundinacea.*

including soup, leather, and tor-
toise-shell, presents serious threats
to many species. Road mortality is
a factor. Some turtles have been
adversely affected by domestic
and feral animals associated with
humans and, in some instances,
by diseases introduced into wild
populations by released pet turtles.

Although the picture is serious,
under the auspices of the World
Conservation Union/Species Survival Commission (IUCN/SSC), a
working group of several hundred
scientists and turtle specialists
have developed and begun to
implement a program for global
turtle recovery. Programs are
underway on all six continents
where turtles live, with each recovery project designed to function within the ecological, cultural,
political, and economic "habitat"
of a particular species. As the success of these individual projects in
large part depends upon local people, each project seeks to provide
incentives to local people to become wise stewards of their turtle
resources. For example, a recovery
project for Madagascar's critically
endangered plowshare tortoise
provides employment and some
technical training for local people,
a market for locally produced
foods and services, and the potential of additional income from eco-
tourism at the field station, since
the project has attracted interna-
tional attention.

———————— ∽ ————————

Turtles are shy creatures, wise-
ly concealing their lives from
our unwelcome scrutiny. David
Carroll has spent decades meticu-
lously observing wild turtles. He
sees natural history with an artful
eye and a strong sense of the
need for conservation. His book
illustrates the joy of observing
animals in their native environment. Conservation programs must
be firmly rooted in a strong
scientific base, but equally important, they must secure a wide base
of popular support at all levels.
The Year of the Turtle will help
generate the popular support
essential to the success of turtle
conservation projects in New
England and around the world.

Michael W. Klemens

*(Dr. Klemens is Director of the IUCN/SSC
global turtle recovery project based at the
American Museum of Natural History in
New York. He has written and lectured
extensively on turtles as well as on the
amphibians and reptiles of New England.)*

INTRODUCTION

This book is about turtles. But it is also about wild places, open space, solitude, and silence. These and other dimensions of the natural world that are fundamental to the human spirit have become harder and harder to hold onto in an increasingly crowded and noisy world.

Not all that long ago the natural world was part of the legacy of every American town, a rich and enriching background of human life. It seems now they never existed, but streams and rivers, ponds and marshes, fields and forests graced every town in the Northeast, and other areas of the country had their corresponding wild places. Over recent decades, too much has been exchanged for far too little, under the notion of the land having to pay for itself. In fact, it owes us nothing; it is we who are deeply indebted to the land. In the nineteenth century Thoreau wrote that the world is "more beautiful than it is useful . . . ." Less than a century and a half later, we have succeeded in making the earth more "useful" than it

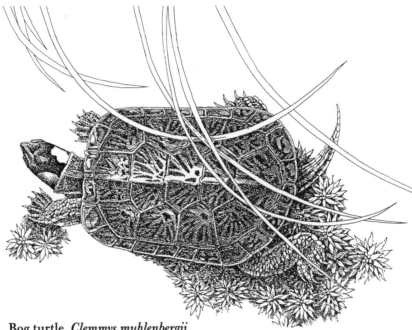

Bog turtle, *Clemmys muhlenbergii.*

is beautiful, our most costly error yet. Thoreauvian economics have never caught on any more than the Native American concept of enjoying the land while owning it not. We divide and divide again each fragment of earth, insisting that it somehow pay for our needs and excesses.

It is my hope that in some way this book can serve as a reminder of what has been, as well as a celebration of what remains. Perhaps it can also serve as an appeal and in some measure an inspiration to a worldwide generation that will have the awareness and will to begin to reverse the tides of human overpopulation and exploitation, and reclaim the natural heritage that has been so sadly and so heedlessly depleted.

Chapter One

EMERGENCE

We need the tonic of wildness,
to wade sometimes in marshes . . .
—Henry David Thoreau

2 April. *The sky is clear tonight, with its myriad stars and nearing full moon. Tomorrow holds the promise of the first sun and warmth of the season, so late in coming this year. It should be a day for turtles; I think they will surely have to end their hibernation, long extended by the unforgiving elements. Recent days of cold rain have been sufficient to dissolve the ice at last and wash away the snow. With the first real sun since the ice is off the marsh, tomorrow will have to be the day of emergence. And I will have to find at least a couple of hours and be there.*

The morning after I make the first notation of the season in my journal, which I hope will signal the end of a prolonged winter and the inception of a steady progress into spring, I set out on my first visit to the swamps, the great marsh around a glacial pond and its environs: the small, winding river with its shrub swamps, sedge meadows, swales, sandy turtle-nesting areas, and surrounding fields and wooded hills. It is a place that I have come to call the Digs. I park my car at the edge of the old logging road and walk to the rusted gate. Long ago it was drawn back for the last time and left open, a beautiful symbol to me. There is nothing on the other side of the dirt road to close this gate against, were one to free it from the earth and grass roots it has settled into. My walking stick is still there from the previous season, leaning into the crevice where the gate is hinged to the granite post, just where I left it after my last wanderings of late October, when I made my farewell visit to the marsh, weeks after the turtles had gone into hibernation.

I take up the gray-white, six-foot staff. This smooth pine branch without any bark feels warm as my fingers curl around it, warm from hours in the strengthening April sun. For months it has measured the cold season's accumulated drifts of snow and glazings of ice, to depths of three to four feet. Now it will serve to measure the water and mud I wade through over the course of another turtle season, to steady me as I make my way through the uncertain underwater terrain that is home to the turtles.

3 April. *Lower 70's, brilliant new sun in the early spring sky, cloudless; slight warm winds with the scent of warming earth come and go. Along the river, redwinged blackbirds calling . . . jet black and flashing red, the males wing among the budding alders. Wood frogs' steady clucking is overlain at intervals with great, shrill spring-peeper choruses that suddenly rise up, build to a deafening crescendo, and then fall back into silence. I pause on the wooden plank bridge to begin recording another round of the seasons of the turtles in my swamp journal, and watch the redwings along the open channel of water, riding the breezes that stir*

in the willows. Just upstream, Blanding's Marsh is filled with the mingled waters of melted snow and spring's first rains, black water with bits of blue, reflected sky against the straw-gold hummocks of last year's tussock sedge.

As I walk along the dirt road to the Swale, I can hear from some distance the ducklike calling of the wood frogs. My excitement rises at the thought of catching the first turtle of the season, especially the prospect of finding a spotted turtle. Only recently have I discovered niches within the complex and interwoven wetlands of the Digs where I can have the expectation of finding this species. Spotted turtles have never been widespread or numerous over the northern fringes of their range; now, with the destruction of so many populations of them, and the severe reduction of their delicate habitats, they are becoming increasingly rare. They are so scarce in some regions where they once were common that they are considered a threatened species.

As I draw near the Swale, my anticipation grows. I begin to see turtles where there are none. I

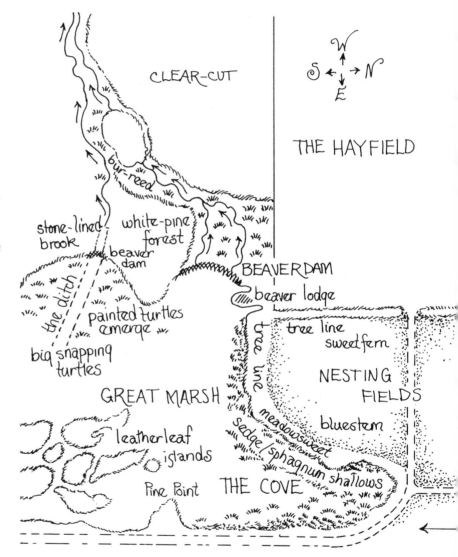

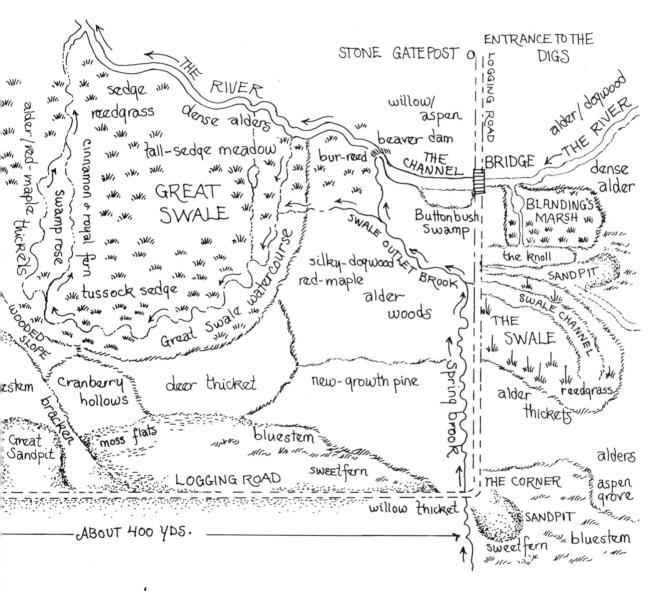

The following labels appear on the map:

STONE GATEPOST ○

ENTRANCE TO THE DIGS

THE RIVER

sedge

reedgrass

dense alders

tall-sedge meadow

bur-reed

willow/ aspen

beaver dam

THE CHANNEL

alder/ dogwood

THE RIVER

LOGGING ROAD

BRIDGE

dense alder

alder/ red-maple thickets

Swamp rose

cinnamon & royal fern

GREAT SWALE

BLANDING'S MARSH

Buttonbush Swamp

the knoll

SANDPIT

tussock sedge

Great Swale watercourse

SWALE OUTLET BROOK

silky-dogwood

red-maple

alder woods

SWALE CHANNEL

THE SWALE

WOODED SLOPE

cranberry hollows

deer thicket

new-growth pine

Spring brook

alder thickets

reedgrass

bluestem

bracken

moss flats

bluestem

Great Sandpit

sweetfern

LOGGING ROAD

THE CORNER

alders

aspen grove

willow thicket

SANDPIT

sweetfern

bluestem

⟵ ABOUT 400 YDS. ⟶

✳ MAP OF THE DIGS ✳

lean on my walking stick and let my eyes move slowly, almost independently, over the wetland before me. The smell of the warming earth alternates with sudden drifts of chill air and watery scents of quick breezes off the Swale. An exhilarating chorus of spring peepers rises up and moves through me; I can feel the chorus as much as hear it. I become lost in the sights and sounds and scents of the awakening spring and can all but taste the season.

My eyes focus on a shadowy movement in one of the rain-filled pools in the dirt road. I come alert, a turtle is on the move. I hurry to the shallow, seasonal pool in time to see the last stirrings of a turtle settling into the mud. Had I not seen the initial movement, I would never have known a turtle lay hidden at my feet. I reach down, finger into the mud, and pull out a spotted turtle.

The turtle, an adult female, withdraws into her shell. I can feel the familiar form of her bottom shell, the orange and black plastron, resting in the palm of my hand. Her wet top shell glistens in the April sun, deep blue-black, with scatterings of lemon-yellow spots in arrangements that suggest constellations in a star-studded sky. I hold her out before me and watch as the water dries from the top of her domed carapace to its margins and her shell takes on the dull luster of a turtle sunning herself, with a high point of reflected sunlight. This moment is a profound keeping of an appointment with the season that has been for months a winter's dream.

The turtle's head, legs, and tail remain tightly drawn within the confines of her shell, the bony armor that has been a key to survival for turtles for an unimaginable span of time. After a while, her forelegs begin to relax and part, revealing her head, which has been drawn even more deeply into the recesses of her shell. A black nose tinged with pale orange gradually emerges from folds of skin formed when she drew in her long neck. Slowly her head extends from the shell and telescopes upward in a graceful, deliberate motion. The turtle blinks . . . even in her blinking there is a slowness and patience. Without

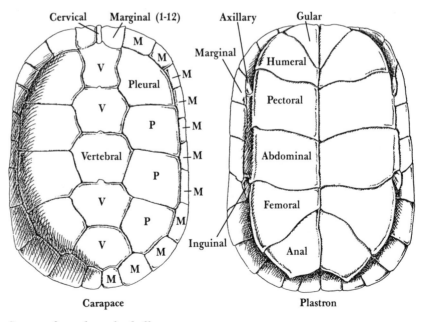

Scutes of pond-turtle shell.

moving her head, she surveys the scene and regards me. To look into the eyes of such a life, a familiar one in its animal beauty, yet so mysterious and so much a separate entity, and to have those eyes look back is an experience that has moved me since I first caught a turtle.

That was many years ago, in a time long lost to me and a swamp that has long since disappeared under blacktop. I was eight years old and thought swamps were forever. I remember clearly the light on the pond that late June evening, the movement in the grassy water plants I now know to be bur-reed; I remember catching and holding and looking into the eyes of that remarkable creature, the first turtle I had ever seen.

I look at this turtle now in my hand and wonder what grace allows me to hold and ponder such a tangible piece of the history of life on earth and, whatever the great separation, of my own life. I take out my small notebook and, gingerly balancing it and the four-inch turtle in my left hand, make a drawing of her carapace and its arrangement of spots, which is different with each spotted turtle. These records of shell patterns allow me to recognize spotted turtles I am

fortunate enough to come upon again. Then I release her where I found her and continue my walk. I may meet this turtle again during nesting season, out on the sandy fields at night, or in some other part of the Digs, years from now.

I leave the marsh at twilight. Rose-gray reflects from every bowl of water held by the earth . . . evening star will have a mirror. Chill air drops into the hollows and quiets the frogs. Wingbeats and whistlings divide the darkening air as a male woodcock takes up his wild, spiralling ascents and reckless, plummeting descents back to earth. In the alder thickets, his intermittent, buzzing calls punctuate the otherwise silent world I leave behind.

12 April, 10 AM. *Low 50's. Brisk, disappointing winds sweep steadily from the northwest across the Digs. Brilliant sun of little avail . . . the sky an almost hurtful blue, too intense on the ruffled waters. Few wood frogs calling in the Swale. Despite the chill in the air, I feel the excitement of entering this realm at turtle season, of having it open up before me as one more time I take up my walking stick and go to the bridge.*

American woodcock, *Philohela minor,* **above alder thicket.**

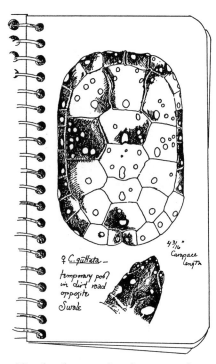

♀ C. guttata —
temporary pool
in dirt road
opposite
Swale

4 3/16"
Carapace
length

Notebook page showing spotted-turtle carapace pattern.

Each time I cross the bridge, I look downstream, where the hour and the mood of the day are reflected in the broad, slow-moving channel that extends one hundred yards or so, then angles off sharply to disappear among the bordering buttonbush and alders. Then I turn and look upstream, where faster-flowing water emerges from a dense, second-growth woodland and slides under the bridge, becoming all but stationary in the channel. I leave the bridge and stealthily approach the Swale. A few intermittent cluckings from wood frogs are the only sign of life I find. It is not a promising day to look for turtles; but once they have emerged from hibernation and begun to breathe again, some may be active even when the season shifts back toward winter. They have their own eagerness for spring. On one of my earliest days of looking for turtles, impatient after the long northern winter, I had gone out to a swamp on a heavily overcast day late in March, with the temperature barely above freezing. As I made my way across the water over a bridge of fallen trees, snow began to fall, the large, wet flakes of an "onion snow." Great white flakes swirling in slow motion through a gray landscape, melting as they landed on logs or the surface of the water. Under clear, cold water, among fallen logs and branches, looking up at me was a spotted turtle, its shell jet black and spots brilliant yellow in the crystal water, the markings on its head and legs glowing orange. I remember the image well: a turtle in the snow.

I continue my walk along the dirt road, which runs a short distance due east, then makes a right-angle turn and runs south to the Great Marsh, a quarter of a mile from the bridge. A short distance beyond the sharp turn, the road passes through an open area of sparsely vegetated, sandy fields. This several-acre plain of impoverished earth is the turtles' primary nesting site and in six or seven weeks will become a scene of great activity. Now it is only beginning to warm, and there is no sign of life in the bleached tufts of bluestem grasses or the stiff twigs of the sweetfern. Bits of eggshells from skunk-raided nests of the previous season are still recognizable scattered among the pebbles on the sandy surface. Mosses and lichens that spread in isolated carpets and colonies show the colors of the turning season. It is their time of year; their deep greens and glowing gray-greens are like the mixtures of malachite and powdered oyster shell used in Oriental paintings. Sparks of brilliant red on the British-soldier lichen accent the landscape out of proportion to their minuteness.

After crossing the fields and passing through a narrow border of aspen, red maple, and white pine, I approach the back end of the marsh and make my way to the beaver dam, a remarkable construction that has altered the landscape and made possible much of this world of the turtles. Built across a drainage channel originally cut by an outlet brook, it turned a small, glacial pond of several acres into a wetland covering scores of acres. The strategic placement of this thirty-yard embankment of interwoven branches and mud replaced a forest with a marsh and provided a habitat for an entirely different spectrum of plants and animals. At this time of year, the water level of the marsh is even with the top of the three-foot-high dam — small spillways run over it to fall into the outlet brook below. When I descend into this shallow brook, I can crouch down and look out across the surface of the water being held back, with a turtle's-eye view of its plane. I wade through the icy runoff, which cuts a clear, narrow stream over white sand, bordered by deep-green banks of moss and arbors of overhanging alders. Ferns are just beginning to thrust out of the thawing earth. Climbing the bank at the other end of the beaver dam, I make my way through the surrounding woods to a high knoll just above grassy coves where I have found newly emerged turtles in past years. The land is open here, a ridge of tall pines with an uncluttered floor of moss and extensive carpets of reindeer lichen. There are few such open areas; with the exception of the nesting fields, the land surrounding the marsh and its tributaries is densely forested.

On this unpromising day, I am rewarded by the sight of the sun glinting off the shells of several turtles basking on grass clumps in the cove below me. They are there, within their own rhythm of the seasons, at their appointed time, taking their appointed place in the all-surrounding landscape. A sign

Beaver dam at Great Marsh.

of spring from a time long before human beings were here to welcome it, turtles appear, and the unique form of their smooth shells reflecting the sun is a landmark of the awakening season, like the swelling buds and the scattered flocks of returning birds.

After looking at the turtles in their place awhile, I roll up my hip waders in preparation for wading in the deeper water of the Great Marsh. Besides insulating against the 38- to 44-degree water, these boots protect me from the extremely painful bite of predaceous diving beetles. They are fully active now, even though the water is cold; I have seen several already in my first looks into the marsh. These excellent swimmers grow to a length of an inch and a half, and while they will not seek

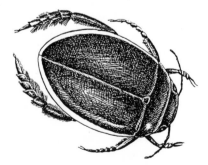

Predaceous diving beetle,
Dytiscidae.

people out to bite them, they can inflict a fiery burning and painful swelling if they become trapped in clothing next to the skin. An even more painful bite can result from inadvertent contact with the much less common giant water bug. In close to forty years of wading swamps and marshes, I have been bitten only twice by such aquatic insects, but each occasion stands out in my mind. High wading boots or, later in the season, old sneakers and high socks with tucked-in trousers protect me from these insects, as well as from the leeches that will come to life as the water warms up. I descend to the water's edge and take my first steps from shore. My feet enter chill water and sink into the mud. Some years there is still snow in the shadows of pines and hemlocks and ice shelves cover most of the marsh when I first wade into the open shallows. The water warms up quickly, however, as the sun penetrates to the black mud bottom. Turtles will be active here.

My feet grow accustomed to the early-season chill, and I begin to make my way among the grass hummocks and small islands of sedges and leatherleaf, and the stumps of large trees that were killed off

when the beavers flooded the forest. In some places, choked with the plant remains of the past summer, the water is quite warm. In others, my feet sink six inches into the mud and reach the cold of the recent winter. The water depth is a fairly constant eight to twelve inches, but the muck is markedly uneven. Even though I have become familiar with many sections of the marsh, the footing is uncertain, and that is reason enough to move slowly. Sometimes one foot reaches down ten or twelve inches and still does not reach a solid bottom, though my bracing foot is firmly planted ankle-deep only a few inches away. I jam my walking stick into the mud, brace my steady leg, and with some effort work my sinking foot free, to test to one side or the other for easier passage, or to retreat and seek a better route.

Some turtles bask on logs, others are hidden, sunning themselves at the edges or in the centers of the hummocks. I see only painted turtles. These are by far the most numerous and most active of the turtles in the marsh; some springs I see over two hundred in one afternoon's searching, thirty or forty on a single fallen tree. In other

Eastern painted turtles, *Chrysemys picta picta,* **sunning themselves.**

years I may encounter only two or three dozen in one day, in the same marsh. If I could be there everyday, I could perhaps understand these patterns better. Some of the sunning turtles are fully alert and dive into the water the instant I make a move. Others wait until I approach quite closely. Their recovery from the stress of hibernation apparently varies and is reflected by their alertness. With minimum stealth, I am able to pick up a few of them before they make a move to escape. One turtle springs into wild and active life when I pick him up, as though my touch awakens him, and he claws at my restraining hand. Even though his eyes were wide open, he seemed to have no awareness of me until I grasped him. What predators might be here, were it not for my presence?

I run my hand over his carapace and feel the warmth it has collected, then look the turtle over and release him. The heat of the sun is still in him, and he swims rapidly in the cold water as he makes his escape. Another turtle remains torpid even after I pick her up. Her back legs remain limp when I touch them or pull at them. There is no sign of injury, and I can detect no outward difference between this individual and the one that just swam away. Her condition could be the result of the long oxygen deprivation of hibernation. I have found several turtles over the years that were partially paralyzed at emergence. Occasionally I have found dead turtles. They seemed to have made it through the winter in good enough condition to emerge but then to have died with no sign of injury or disease. My urge is to take the turtle home, to try to save her. But I am an observer. I place her back in the swirls of dried grass where she had been, out of the wind, on a warming bit

Redwinged blackbird, *Agelaius phoeniceus.*

of earth. One cannot always intervene. Perhaps the heat of the sun and the actions of her own respiration will restore her.

I move on, checking out the hummocks. Occasionally I hear the rustling of a turtle as it scrambles from its hidden solarium in the grass, followed by the characteristic splash as it falls into the water. The ungraceful dive is followed by a rapid, quite graceful swim to the bottom in search of a hiding place, which can be the mud itself, an underwater log or

tangle of branches, or the matted strands at the base of a clump of sedges. Early in the season the water is open, the great growth of water plants has not begun, and turtles have to swim greater distances to find cover. They are more exposed, and therefore more cautious, even when in water. Once a turtle finds an underwater hiding place, he can stay there a long time. At the height of summer, a turtle can stay under for an hour or more with no great strain; inactive, in the colder waters of spring, a turtle can go hours without surfacing.

I come to the edge of a deep channel that bisects the otherwise shallow cove with its scores of grassy islands. It is one of the few deepwater areas in all of the marsh, except where the marsh joins the pond proper. This channel runs on a straight line from the shore, some fifty yards out into the water, and its sheared perpendicular banks drop to a floor that is five feet below the overall water level of the surrounding marsh. Directly behind it, all but hidden in the woods, is a stone-lined brook. Beavers have constructed a small dam across this channel, which was originally dug by humans to

drain a meadow. Before that, there was a forest here; it was felled by humans who opened up a meadow. In time, the meadow was abandoned, and over more time, the forest moved back in and reclaimed a grassland. With a dam constructed at the same low drainage point chosen by humans, beavers reversed the draining process, drowned a forest, and created a marsh. If hayfields become important enough again, humans could open up the beaver dam, draining the marsh and re-establishing a meadow.

The channel is too deep for me to wade across, so I work my way along its margin and stop where the mud becomes too deep to pass through. Here I survey the marsh. Out of the mixed panorama of sky and distant hills, the wind-rippled water farther out, the dead trees and grassy islands with their reflections in the still water before me, a single image begins to form in my mind, unconsciously at first. At the edge of a pile of tangled branches a smooth form reaches from the water in a low arc. It is the shell of a snapping turtle. Immediately, as this recognition comes to me, I see the dark triangular head protruding from the water, more than a foot in front of the shell. The turtle is enormous. This vision seems to have suddenly appeared before me, but both his head and shell are dry—the turtle has been watching me for some time. A chill of excitement comes over me as I look at the turtle and consider catching him. Over my years in the swamps, I have caught many large snappers, but I know that only one was equal to the turtle before me now, and that one weighed forty-six pounds.

The turtle and I look at each other. I would have to cross several yards of deep, soft mud to reach him. This is more his realm than mine. It might be better for me to stay in my role of observer. Were I to get hold of that creature, I would have a struggle on my hands just trying to drag him back to more solid footing where I could take a good look at him. It would be extremely difficult to get him on shore, and I have no camera with me, nor anyone to show him to. But I am drawn to feel the strength of this great turtle, to haul him at least partway out of the water and appreciate the size and primeval beauty of this lord of the waterways. I would not

hesitate were the turtle not quite so large, the footing so uncertain. The Great Marsh seems more wild and alone than ever now, more timeless and otherworldly, with this ancient snapping turtle as its focus. With that same reptilian stare now regarding me, he could have been a turtle of long ago watching the movements of a long-vanished dinosaur in a swamp that is now a mountain range.

Apprehension mingles with excitement as I move a slow half step to the edge of the last grass hummocks and look for footing in the open water I will have to cross to reach the turtle. There before me, lying on the bottom in less than a foot of water, is a second tremendous snapping turtle. In the clear water, his enormous shell is a deep-blue slate-gray, and his partially withdrawn head appears the same. I have never seen such color in a snapping turtle. It may be a quality of great age or due to this turtle's recent emergence from hibernation. All of the green-black mossy growth common on the shells of these highly aquatic turtles has died off over the winter, and his carapace has not taken on the dark muddy tones I am so familiar with. The turtle glows like

malachite in the water. I check across the pool. The first turtle has not moved. I look down at the one below me, his head and legs in a stationary crouch, his thick, spiked tail extending straight out from the jagged rear edge of his carapace. I press my walking stick into the mud; I will need both hands.

I step off the underwater ledge into the deeper water behind the turtle, who has not yet made a move. He will go into action the instant I touch him. Extending both my hands slowly beneath the surface, I reach to encircle the turtle's thick tail, thankful that the water is clear and I can see exactly where his head and tail lie. The placement of a snapping turtle's eyes is such that I can see into them from my position directly over him. Without taking my eyes from his, I put my hands around the base of his tail—I can barely reach around it.

The instant I take my grip, the turtle surges forward, head lunging, all four legs thrusting. The placid surface becomes a churning sea of mud and water, my sweatshirt is thoroughly splattered. Even in his tail I can feel the power of this animal. I grasp hard against the armorlike scales and sharp spikes of his tail, trying to keep my knuckles from the triangular marginal plates at the rear edge of his carapace, which are like the teeth of a crosscut saw. As he struggles forward, the turtle pulls his tail against my hold, first to one side, then to the other. I set my feet in the mud and pull him toward me. I feel behind me with one foot, set it, then follow with my other foot, struggling backward to the shallows of the grass hummocks, where I hope to beach this beautiful creature. The snapper does not turn and strike; in this depth, with open water before him, all his actions are set upon escape.

There is no lifting this thrashing turtle from the water; I can barely drag him backward, against his great strength and resolute will, to some landing place. I step back and get one foot up on the marshy bank behind me, a laborious step from the deep mud onto the less than solid ground that is my only retreat. I move my other foot up and struggle backward into the grass clumps. As I work the turtle up into these shallows, he gains a hold on their turfy margin and becomes twice as strong, pulling me forward and down on one knee.

Getting back on my feet, I wrestle him further into the hummocks. I cannot lift him, or straighten up myself, but merely hold him in place at the edge of the sedge growth. I keep my grip but stop pulling. The snapper seizes the rim of the submarine turf with his powerful forefeet, sinking two-inch claws into the mass of mud and roots, and sets his equally strong, sharp-clawed hindfeet. He has taken his hold. After the thrashing, swirling struggle, we are both still. The roiled water settles into a mirror. In the silence I can hear the turtle breathing.

It could be argued whether or not I have "caught" a turtle. We share the exhaustion. The snapper's long, powerful neck is withdrawn, his massive head rests at eye level in the water; he looks straight ahead, across the broad expanse of the marsh. With the remarkably slow motion that these creatures are capable of, he moves his head forward. His neck appears at the fore edge of his broad carapace. Moving almost like a separate creature, his head glides in a measured turn on his arching neck, along the water surface, back to face me. I look into those impressive eyes: a white fleck of

Eye of a snapping turtle, *Chelydra serpentina.*

daylight shows in the gold-ringed, jet-black pupil from which five black slashes radiate on a ground of amber and blue scattered with black dots. There is a distance in them, a coldness; they are eyes filled with stars. I look into them and look back into an unfathomable time and point of consciousness. It may be in such eyes that the universe first discovered a way to look back upon itself.

Millennia after millennia, the earth has been looked at through turtle eyes. There were turtle eyes to reflect the sky, land, and water of this planet nearly two hundred million years ago. As with many of the living forms that have appeared on earth, the origins of Chelonia (the order that comprises turtles) are obscure. It is unclear how, out of the flow of life from fish to amphibians to early reptiles, there came to be turtles. Suddenly they are there, fully formed, in the fossil record, that incomplete history of life on earth that paleontologists, with time-hindered perspectives, strive to read. The earliest turtles have been found in deposits dating back over one hundred eighty million years. Proganochelys, the most ancient chelonian, could not retract his head and had small teeth, but he carried a bony shell and was unmistakably a turtle.

With the appearance of this bony shell, a feature completely different from anything that had evolved in any other vertebrate was introduced. It was a remarkable development that had come to stay. Turtles made adjustments to the extreme restructuring of the vertebrate skeleton that this shell represented. With backbones and ribs encased in specialized bony layers enclosing not only their lungs and viscera, but also their shoulder and pelvic girdles, they had to develop a new way of breathing and walking. In the individual turtle, the skeletal rearrangement that results in the enclosing shell comes about as a result of changes in the migratory pathway taken by certain embryonic cells. This new pathway takes cells laterally to form the carapace instead of bellyward to meet the breastbone, as it does in all other vertebrates including the distant relatives of turtles. The skeletons of all other animals with backbones—from giraffes to salamanders—are very similar. Only the turtle departs from this universal design.

Although the first turtles were not able to withdraw their heads into their wonderful, protecting shells, early descendants came up with ways to do just that. A suborder called Pleurodira, arriving closely on the heels of Proganochelys, devised a method of pulling their heads sideways into their shells. Fifty species of these side-necked turtles, all of which are confined to the southern land masses, inhabit the world today. Another method was developed by the second (and only other) suborder, the Cryptodirans, which somewhere around the same time evolved a manner of withdrawing their heads deep into their shells by retracting their necks in an S-shaped curve. All North American turtles belong to this group, the "hidden-necked" turtles. With these changes, accomplished some one hundred fifty million years ago, turtles had essentially completed their modernization program. After an initial period of radical and rapid adaptive radiation, these animals shunned further dramatic innovation and, adhering to a design that proved capable of withstanding an unprecedented test of time among the higher vertebrates, came to be the remarkably unchanged turtles of the present world.

Among the glimpses back in time that fossils provide, to points so remote they seem to have occurred on another world, is one that reveals turtles we would recognize just as easily as we recognize the ones we see today. They appear, in that misty glimpse, as semi-aquatic marsh-dwellers of the late Triassic period, around one hundred eighty million years ago. Turtles did well in those early marshes, which themselves shifted continually over the face of a changing planet, disappearing here, reforming there, as mountain ranges and seas traded places and the very continents moved about. The ancestral turtles took on varied shapes as they moved in that mysterious and generally gradual transformation known as evolution. Some became entirely terrestrial and inhabited forests, grasslands, and deserts. Others became more and more aquatic and moved to deeper bodies of freshwater—the lakes, rivers, and ponds of a distant time. Still others returned to the sea itself, the vast saline home of their progenitors . . . and the progenitors of everything that lives on the planet earth today. Yet with all their adaptations to eternally changing climates and terrains, and their interactions with remarkably varied plants and animals over time, turtles have remained turtles.

Chelonian history is such that a "modern" turtle, the softshell, has been found in fossil deposits of the mid-Cretaceous period—about one hundred million years ago. At the same time that Archelon, with his twelve-foot carapace, was swimming in the warm shallows of the Nio-bara Sea (now a dry area of the central plains of the United States, extending from South Dakota to Texas), softshell turtles like the ones that are with us today were shuffling into the sand and silt bottoms of waterways that have long since vanished. Although they were already well established at a time when the early mammals were just beginning their development into a major group of animals, softshells represent a highly specialized application of the basic chelonian plan, a high-

tech version that flourishes today in its same one-hundred-million-year-old manner in the temperate regions of Asia, Africa, and North America. Few forms and functions remain unchanged over such a span of time without becoming outmoded to the point of extinction.

The times, places, and specific forms of turtles have undergone their share of changes, but the basic chelonian design has remained unaltered since its first sudden appearance. (Meiolania, a turtle with a horned skull, carried some early turtle features almost to the present day, having become extinct only twenty thousand years ago.) As unique and successful as it has proven to be, the shell is not the only thing these animals have going for them. As a group, they have adapted to a wide range of habitats. There are chelonians that are able to feed on cacti in desert sands, and others that can live beneath the sea, feeding on sponges composed mostly of silica—which is like spun glass.

With all their capability for endurance, turtles have not escaped extinction. When the most recent widespread occurrence of this phenomenon passed over the earth sixty-five million years ago and

Spotted turtle, *Clemmys guttata*, withdrawn into shell.

carried away the dinosaurs forever, many species of turtles went with them. Among those lost were Archelon and other marine turtles that shared the seas with him. But in the face of the forces that have ended many living lines, the overall turtle solution has held. Even today, when they are under severe stress from the great new pressure represented by people and their activities, there are about two hundred twenty-five species of living turtles. When doors closed on the dinosaurs, turtles found openings. As the earth's uneasy geology and restless climate changed the physical terms of existence, and phenomena such as the appearance of flowering plants and the emergence of mammals brought profound pressure on the directions life could take, turtles slipped among the primitive ferns and newly evolved grasses and eluded their historic as well as their previously unknown predators. Turtle populations ebbed and flowed with the abiotic and biotic upheavals and found margins in time and space in which to keep going. When creatures as enormous as brontosaurus and as minute as marine phytoplankton came to their limits and could move

no farther along time's mysterious channel, turtles continued.

The living bit of prehistoric life I now hold in my hands shifts his position slightly. We look at each other awhile. Then, in measured slow motion, he slides his head to the front edge of his carapace and, neck withdrawn, once again looks straight ahead out over the water. I decide to pull him toward me, higher up onto the grassy shallows. The moment my hands tighten on the massive base of his tail, he thrusts all four legs against the turf and lashes straight out with a lightning strike of head and searing jaws—the *smack!* can be heard across the marsh. Immediately following this instinctive, unfocused strike, the turtle gains leverage with his thick-muscled forelegs and strains to turn and face his tormentor. A snapping turtle cornered on land, or in shallow water with no escape route, will keep turning in a tight circle to face any challenger, with neck and legs set for a strike and jaws slightly apart. These creatures will not back down.

I work against his counterclockwise turning, forcing his tail and rear edge of his shell in the opposite direction. It takes great effort to countermand this ani-

mal's determined advance. The snapper unleashes an awesome strike back along the edge of his shell: a frighteningly impressive demonstration of his power and reach. My hands are safe from those jaws, at the base of his tail and along the rear margin of his shell, but my knuckles are scraped and cut from the jagged plates at the back edge of his carapace. Snappers must be handled by the base of the tail or the very edge of the carapace, for they can extend their heads and necks far back along the sides, or even top, of their shells. Also, large snappers can be injured if carried by the tail and must be supported or managed by the back end of the shell. If I were to lift him, I would not be able to hold this massive turtle far enough away from my body to keep my legs safe from his slashing jaws. He is greatly agitated now, and like an arm-locked wrestler struggles to come at me, to break my hold. My arms grow tired, and I have inconvenienced this great beast enough. I had wanted to have a good look at him, to feel his strength. All of the energy and power in the thrusting force of his neck and driving strength of his legs are transmitted to me through my two hands gripping the base of his tail. The life that moves in the weight of this turtle makes him seem even larger than he is—and he must weigh close to fifty pounds. I plan a backward move from my position of one foot planted, one knee braced in the water, and let go.

The turtle rotates halfway around to face me, then stops. Aware of his release, he settles slowly down on his legs, plastron to the bottom. He is so big that nearly all of him is visible above the ankle-deep water. I stand motionless after rising stiffly from my long crouch in the chill water and withdrawing a step. The time and place will not allow a drawing, and I regret I have no camera with me. The turtle regards me with one eye, the other looks to the open water beyond the marshy ledge. He waits. I continue to stand completely still.

I always wonder at such moments what turtle intelligence is at work, what blend of consciousness and instinct inherited from a time long past moves through the animal's ancient mind. What does he read in the scene and situation before him? He reads the hour and the event, the water and the light, in a manner as mysterious as a migratory bird's reading of the star formations in the night's black sky.

The turtle slowly pushes out from the protective shield of his carapace with his left foreleg, almost imperceptibly setting it against a firm tussock. Then he makes his move. With a powerful thrust of that left foreleg and a great pull from the right foreleg he turns his great mass toward the open marsh and propels himself off the ledge, into the water. With alternate strokes of foreleg and hindleg, he churns across the muddy bottom. A wide swath of thousands of tiny bubbles rises to the surface along the submarine route of the disappearing turtle as he heads for the safety of the deeper channel.

I look back to where I had seen the first turtle and am surprised to see that he has not moved, though he was doubtless aware of the struggle that just took place thirty feet from where he lay, his head and the top of his carapace barely above the surface. It is such a remarkable moment, this discovery of two magnificent snapping turtles in the open waters of early spring, that I decide to try to capture the second animal. Many years may well pass before I encounter even one other such extraordinary turtle, if I ever do at all. I feel an unavoidable uneasiness as I step once more from the relatively solid masses of grass tussocks into the yielding muck and begin the crossing. The turtle knows that my approach does not bode well. He slowly withdraws his head and begins to stir in the mud with all four legs. I struggle through the deep and difficult muck as quickly as I can. His shell is sinking straight down into the mud.

No one passes this way. These two turtles rarely, perhaps never, come into contact with human activity in this setting, and for decades there has been nothing for these masters of their environment to flee from. With nothing to challenge them, they have not had to practice an escape since they were only a few inches long, when sudden submergence in the mud might mean survival. When larger snappers do feel the need to disappear, they still have a remarkable ability to do so, however. I once saw an adult in six feet of clear lake water vanish into the bottom in what seemed an instant, without stirring up a wisp of mud.

I have kept a constant eye on what I calculated to be the location of the turtle's tail as I approached, and now I reach down into the roiled water, grope in the mud for the rear edge of his shell, and seize him at the base of the tail. It is immediately clear to me that this snapping turtle is just as big as the first—I am in no position to calculate minute differences in weight or temperament. There is no way to heave this equally resisting giant to anything resembling terra firma. I wrest him out of the mud and water and draw him up over a half-submerged log, balancing him there for something of a look. As with the first, this turtle puts off his struggling for a moment and rests his massive head at the water surface. Then he explodes into action, strains against the log with forefeet, sprays water with stroking hindfeet, and rapidly fires several lunging, snapping strikes at the world in general. I let go. The turtle lunges forward and sets off in a wide arc around the site of our encounter. Then he plows rapidly across the bottom to the same deep channel in which the first turtle took refuge, leaving his own wide trail of bubbles on the quieting surface of the marsh.

Snapping turtles are rightly known as formidable creatures. Although accounts of their biting, as of their size and other attributes, are often exaggerated out of pure snapping-turtle aura, even a five- or ten-pound individual makes quite an impression and seems to be twice as big as he really is. It is startling to feel the strength of a snapping turtle with a carapace of only four or five inches as he tries to free himself from a restraining hand—the entire turtle feels like muscle and energy, pure force in living form. Though many people claim to have seen snappers as big as kitchen tables, only rare individual turtles reach or slightly exceed a straight-line carapace length of a foot and a half and a weight of seventy to eighty pounds. Once the tremendous mass of the head and the powerful length of the neck, tail, and legs are added in, the creature is great enough. A forty-six-pound turtle I once managed to bring home for a photography session reached from one end of the bathtub to the other, from nostril to tail tip, and in the end managed to climb out of the tub.

The vile temperament associated with these reptiles largely results from provocation by human beings, the latter making the situation confrontational. Left with an unimpeded view of the horizon, especially if water is within reach, the turtle will rise on his feet, shell high above the earth, tail sloping down and dragging behind, and move off with a deliberate, stalking stride that inspires images of dinosaurs. Cornered, headed off from the water, approached or restrained, the turtle will lash out with legendary speed and terrific force, his head and neck becoming lethal weapons. These turtles will not attack, but neither will they back down. Unlike most turtles, snappers do not rely on enclosure in a shell and passive defense. Their plastrons have been reduced to a narrow cross of bone that covers less than a sumo wrestler's thong does, offering little protection but allowing great freedom of action. The carapace is used more as a shield, from beneath which the head is thrown like a retrievable lance, than as the bony fortress into which turtles of most species retreat. (Another turtle without the typical chelonian armor is the softshell, and it, too, features a long neck, cutting jaws, raking claws, and sudden movement. Accounts in the literature nearly all bear out my own experiences with snapping turtles: they do not bite when in the water, even if interfered with; but one would be reluctant to prove this comforting generalization wrong. Certainly if any opening is left to them, these wild and impressive animals will avail themselves of it and move along their own way.

In my more intrepid youth, I slid along in the water on my belly, reaching under lily pads and into the mud as I searched for turtles, a technique I labelled "groping." Twice I had the experience of placing my hand on the mossy back of a snapping turtle, submerged and still, waiting in ambush for something a good deal smaller than me to come along. On one occasion, the turtle moved off, no happier to have a strange creature come out of nowhere and rest upon it than I was to suddenly feel my hand pressing upon that unmistakable algae-covered carapace. On the other occasion, the turtle remained motionless, and I slid off through the water to investigate another part of the swamp. These turtles,

after attaining any noticeable size, are used to being left alone and have deservedly come to expect it.

I have been bitten by a snapping turtle only once, and that was by the first one I ever caught. My own ignorance and carelessness were the contributing factors. I was ten or eleven years old and had seen the turtle several times in various parts of my favorite swamp; I had found him two or three times lurking under a floating board in shallow water. I would poke the board gently with a stick, to send it floating aside, and reveal the snapper lying on the bottom. The turtle's eyes would rotate slowly upward in his motionless head to regard me. Not pleased with the image I presented, towering above the water, and unsettled at being revealed to the afternoon's penetrating light, the turtle would almost magically shuffle to the side, with no real apparent movement, and disappear beneath the board once more. I would let it go at that. The turtle was not all that large compared with many I was to know in the future, but he was an adult and awesome enough for a boy who had handled only spotted and painted turtles in the wild. One day I set aside my ner-

vousness and decided to catch the snapper. I was shaking with excitement but managed the grabbing and dragging ashore all right. I stood back and looked at that mysterious and frightening creature with a reverence that has never left me, though the youthful fear has abated.

I then made a painful mistake. Wanting to witness more of the impressive, blinding speed, and the sight and sound of the lunging strike and snap that had accompanied the turtle's reluctant drag from the swamp, I took a stick and moved it toward his great head. I never saw the strike. The turtle's razor jaws slashed across three fingers, opening cuts in all of them. Stunned, I contemplated my bleeding fingers as the turtle headed back to the swamp. In less than an instant, he had struck, cut, and released my menacing hand in order to turn in the direction of his desired safety and freedom. He did not hold on until it thundered, luckily for me. Snappers under stress will at times cling with bulldog tenacity. Although reports of them holding on forever are part of the lore that has accumulated around these animals, reliable statements of those who have had a more violent relationship with snapping turtles than I have indicate that even severed heads will maintain their hold. These maligned turtles, who cling so tenaciously to existence, should be left the time and the space they deserve. They do seem more capable than most of earth's plants and animals of surviving the assaults, direct and indirect, of the recent arrival, *Homo sapiens,* who seems more and more to have come as an intruder. Snapping turtles, embodiments of turtles who shared the earth with the dinosaurs for a time and are now obliged to share it with the human species, might well report that the former companions were far less stressful.

12 April, 4:30 PM. *Winds all the more brisk as I walk from the Great Marsh and pass along the sandy nesting fields back to the Swale. The season seems to turn and run backward on the restless blasts of air . . . land, earth, and water seem equally unsettled. Except for ceaseless rustlings in the reedgrass and the steady sweep of wind, the Swale is silent. I miss the frogs who greeted my arrival. Standing on a dry point of the flooded logging road at the edge of the Swale, I lean on my walking stick, hunch my shoulders against the chill, and whistle a series of sharp, imitation peep-frog calls, as loudly as I can, into the wind. After several minutes of my own shrill whistles, a call comes back, and then another and another. The rolling clucks of wood frogs join in. Single notes and series ring out above the soughing in the pines, the clicking and swishing in the alder branches. A chorus rises up and for a few minutes displaces all other sound. Then the March-like wind takes over the silence again as the frogs give up their singing. My heart is gladdened. Hidden and silent, they are there, thousands of them.*

13 April. *47 degrees. Still, with intermittent light showers of widely spaced raindrops . . . chill off the water and out of the low pockets in the alder groves, which not long ago held the last of the snow. To the Digs, 3:30 PM.*

I hear a kingfisher in the distance, then see one fly along the river, out beyond Blanding's Marsh. I make a search along shore . . . nothing astir. I note a small oval area of freshly dug-up sandy mud on the bottom, only inches out from the bank, and dig down. Something had burrowed or dug in that spot; all around it is the dark bottom with sunken leaves and interlaced grass and sedge. The coldness of the water comes to me . . . my hand grows numb almost at once as I work my fingers into the muck, and I cannot endure the aching cold for more than ten seconds. This brings me a very tangible realization of why little is on the move, even if the ice has retreated and the sun has shone for a few days late in March and into mid-April. I regret that I do not have a battery of thermometers to record earth,

Spring peepers, *Hyla crucifer*.

air, and water temperatures—even the temperatures of the turtles themselves—on my excursions. But it is safe to say that the water is cold. A few weeks into the season it seems little more than melted ice.

I move on toward the Swale and startle up a flock of common grackles from the outlet brook that cuts across the dirt road. The dark birds were along the brooklet's sandy margins and at the

Common grackles, *Quiscalus quiscula,* in a thicket.

bases of the alders where the run-off spreads and wanders once it has crossed the road. I think that they had discovered the countless larvae lining this tiny current and were feasting on them. These flat, long-tailed swimmers, which I have seen undulating in all directions throughout the spring flood waters, are mayfly larvae. They cannot move upstream against the swiftly running water at its point of crossing the road, so they work along its wet margin, some essentially on land as they wriggle over glistening sand. There are places where they form thick, living aggregates, and these must constitute worthwhile food for the large, lean, spring grackles.

It interests me that this is an unmixed flock of grackles, not one among them a member of the other blackbird tribes that always seem to travel together. With a flurry of midnight wings they flew up into the higher branches of the alder thicket and its several red maples. There they took up their characteristic positions, dark shapes against the silvery lit, gray sky of early spring. I stand still, and they go on singing, if that is the proper word for their intriguing cacophony. Something reminiscent

of the remarkable rolling call of the bobolink can be detected, and a blackbird-like, raucous, yet not unmelodious, wall of sound rises up. For about ten minutes they continue, without a single silent pause for breath. I content myself to enjoy this unique ensemble and search the open water and masses of submerged reedgrass for some sign of stirring. This might be the highlight of my visit to the Digs, and it feels pleasing to be here in the silver chill and rain and stillness of a day at the season's changing, listening to grackles.

15 April, 1:30 PM. *Sun and mistlike clouds exchanging possession of the sky with its chill eastern wind. Temperature varying widely with the alternate appearance and disappearance of the sun and the thickness of the clouds. I pass by the cove of the Great Marsh, where the wind is most free to roam and carries a penetrating oceanic edge though I am seventy miles inland. It is an unfamiliar wind I work against as I walk toward the marsh, for it is nearly always at my back on this approach to the water, sweeping down from the mountain behind me, from the west-northwest.*

I leave the marsh to the great blue heron that lifts in silence out of the shallows of the cove and sweeps away, low against the steady drift of air, across the open water and stretches of islands formed by stands of leatherleaf. I cross the sandy fields and walk out into the long, narrow hayfield. Though it is mid-April, the season is yet balanced on the edge of emergence, for the month has been almost completely bereft of sun or warmth. I am eager to find another spotted turtle, and thereby another clue as to where they hibernate in this complex, many-faceted ecosystem. I am drawn to explore the alder zone bordering the acres and acres of sedge meadow and its small meandering streams that diverge from the little river to wind among the tussocks and eventually rejoin it. I had discovered this realm on an earlier excursion when I followed the main river downstream from the bridge, wading along beaver and muskrat channels that thread among the alder thickets and emergent buttonbush. I named this the Great Swale. A short distance out across the open plane of the hayfield, I turn to my right and pass through a thin band of tall white pines that line the high ground at the field's edge, circle a dead oak, and descend a slope of several yards that drops into an entirely different world.

I have left dry ground behind me. My feet sink into sphagnum and muck as I walk the landward border of the all but endless alder thickets, seeking some route to explore my way through them and eventually to the open realm of the sedge meadow. The long slender trunks of the alders extend in dense profusion, reaching horizontally and vertically, interweaving, crisscrossing, from the land or water surface up to twenty feet or so. Even when leafless, they weave a woody fabric in space that I cannot see through, let alone move through. No one place is easier than any other for my passage, but at length I fix my eyes on an up-reaching alder as far ahead as I can see and begin working my way to it. At times I am held in place, snared by the tenacious thorns of the swamp rose. Every few yards are slowly gained. My walking stick is no good here; I draw it behind me for eventual use in more open space, as I literally climb through the landscape. Where the water

Alder thicket, *Alnus rugosa*, Great Swale.

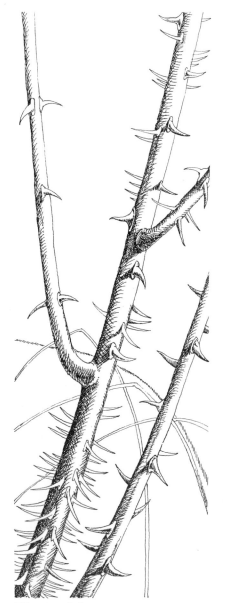

Thorns of the swamp rose.

lies deeper, the alder clumps are a bit more widely spaced, and I keep to these circuitous channels, sidling around and between tree stands. There are now mounds formed by royal fern, cinnamon fern, and tussock sedge among the alders. These are covered with the fallen wreckage of the previous year's growth, and only the sedges' short, sharp spears of gray-green show any renewed life for the spring. I keep to my straight-ahead plan, searching every plant form that reaches from the water, which varies from four inches to eighteen inches in depth. I edge my way around the various mounds—it would be impossible to step from one to another of these islands, even at this early stage of the season, when so much is yet to fill in. As I move through the narrow mud-and-water passageways, many of the mounds around me are waist high at their summits. Once unfurled, and at the height of their summer growth, the ferns here will tower over me.

There is no canopy. The sun filters in through the reddish upper alder branches, where catkins droop now, releasing clouds of yellow-green pollen when I jolt against the sinuous up-reaching

trunks. The sun falls on these maroon-gray trunks with their speckles of white lenticels and on the burnt-out umbers and ochers, black and silvery whites, and straw-golds of last year's alder and red-maple leaves, crumbled fern fronds, and masses of interwoven sedges and grasses. Here in the somber golds and earth tones of piles of spent growth that collect among the tree trunks and stiff, persistent fern shafts, I look for turtles.

And here I find one. After nearly two hours of searching numberless niches in an area I had never traversed in my explorations of this wild place, I look down and suddenly see the top of a spotted turtle's shell showing through a layer of dry leaves. I had felt right about this place as I made my slow search of it and had imagined a turtle here or a turtle there in a propitious spot reached by the sunlight.

Down in the top layer of fallen leaves and ferns, close to earth formed by the raised bases of young red maples and well-established royal ferns, she had found warmth early in the turtle season. Low and out of the wind, her shell could collect heat from the sun, even when it was veiled by thin clouds. And by half hiding herself in this cryptic basking (which I have observed primarily in spotted turtles), she would not be likely to be discovered. Farther to the south, years ago, in red-maple and alder swamps of coastal New England that are now long vanished, I commonly found spotted turtles sunning themselves this way at the earliest turning toward spring. Even hatchlings would hide under dried grass or among cranberry vines, almost out of sight but well within reach of the sun's heat.

The surrounding water is numbing cold, the air sweeping around my face and shoulders is chill; but out of the wind and water, in a protected solarium, the turtle has built up a temperature in the 70-degree range and feels noticeably warmer than the hand that picks her up from the leaves. The turtle is an ectotherm; her body temperature is determined by environmental factors outside her body, as is the case with all living herptiles, the reptiles and amphibians. The turtle observer is an endotherm, meaning that his body temperature is primarily controlled by physiological processes within his body, as is the case

with mammals and birds. In the environmental situation of the moment, the ectotherm seems to enjoy an all-pervasive warmth greater than that of the occasionally shivering endotherm — the turtle's sun-warmed shell seems to warm my hand. At various points in my slow wading of the icy water, I would stop to take advantage of a lull in the swirling wind or a strengthening in the sun, pull my arms close to my body, and turtle-like, try to collect some warmth from my surroundings.

The term *cold-blooded* is something of a misnomer when applied to turtles and other ectotherms. By their movements over days and seasons, and selections of different niches within their environment, they are capable of great temperature control. Turtles can take in heat and raise their metabolic rate when necessary for such physiological functions as digestion, growth, and reproduction during the season of peak activity; at the other end of the year they are able to thermoregulate downward to a point barely above freezing and sustain life throughout the long cold season. They are able to take up heat from the earth or other substrate on which they rest,

or from the water that surrounds them, and become warmer than the air. The best way for a turtle to warm itself is to bask, and this is an especially critical activity for most temperate species at their time of emergence. Long before they require food, turtles need heat from the strengthening spring sun. It awakens the dormant flicker of life that has been held within them all winter long.

Turtles have different styles of sunning themselves. The great snapping turtles I came upon earlier in the week were basking in shallow water, lying just above or just below the surface, which is common among these large turtles. They will occasionally haul themselves out on a raft of branches at the water's edge or even onto a rock in a river. A species as aquatic as the snapper, musk turtles also will bask barely beneath the water surface, lying on the mud or a submerged log. But these small and rather ungainly turtles are agile and surprisingly strong climbers; they will ascend on occasion to the most difficult and precipitous branches reaching high out of the water to take their sun. When disturbed, they launch themselves from considerable heights with no thought at all of grace, dropping like stones into the protecting depths below. When turtles such as these, which live almost entirely underwater, do come up to bask, they are drying out and discouraging such aquatic pests as parasites and leeches in addition to warming themselves up. Softshells, perhaps the best-swimming and most aquatically adapted of freshwater turtles, are extremely fond of basking. They climb logs or other perches to dry out their leathery shells, extending long necks and flipperlike feet in graceful abandon, their poses taking on a balletic air.

Because they are the most numerous, and conceal their love of the sun the least, the most familiar baskers are the painted turtles. They line exposed logs by the dozens and sometimes pile up two or three deep when sunning spaces are limited. These turtles seem confident of their wariness, quickness, and swimming ability and usually make little attempt to be hidden about their sunning practices. During early periods of emergence, however, even this species is apt to be cryptic about basking. The stress of the long hibernation, the low water and air temperatures that restrict their activity levels, and the lack of cover in a wetland habitat devoid of vegetation, prompt them to be cautious. They often lie in dense tufts of the previous year's growth or low in a secluded spot at water's edge, on a log or the warming earth itself. Turtles need sunlight to metabolize vitamins in their diet; their extensions of head, neck, legs, and feet (which are often turned over, bottoms to the sun) facilitate this and add an elaborate quality to their poses. Even the more terrestrial species, the box and wood turtles, will sun themselves, in a spotlight of sun in a forest grove or at the edge of a field or road, particularly during spring. I have seen wood turtles, recently out of the icy streams in which they hibernate, climb in among tangles of fallen alder trunks and dried grasses and angle their shells to best advantage to take the April sun that floods down through trees that have yet to leaf out.

The turtle among the leaves was encased in her shell when I found her, and she drew herself more tightly within when I reached down and picked her up. After a time, she cautiously extends her head and neck. She has only recently emerged from hibernation. This may be her first day of active life in the new season, and I am certain that she has passed the long winter beneath this very mound, down in the mud under about ten inches of water, in a pocket hidden among creeping, twisting fern rhizomes and tangled roots of alder and red maple. With the air and water temperatures what they have been, she cannot have moved far from where she passed the winter. The first weeks of the turtle season have yielded me the discovery of a spotted turtle's hibernaculum. I will take her home so that I can do drawings and watercolors of her, and I'll release her as the season warms, before the breeding begins. I try to familiarize myself with some immediate aspect of the trackless swamp thicket. The turtle I have caught knows this area well, no doubt, and I want to release her as near as possible to the exact spot in which I found her. There are no signs here, so I take an empty seed packet from my shirt pocket and fix it on a small branch. It will leave no permanent impression on the wilderness and in fact will probably be blown away before I return; but it may serve as a small sign to help me pinpoint the spotted turtle's basking mound when I bring her back. In the distance I can make out whitened branches against the sky, the dead crown of a red oak just below the hayfield. I head that way, back to higher ground.

———————— 〜 ————————

The melting had been slow this year, but at length the last wet snows of mid and late March had led to the first rains of early April. Ice receded from the shallow shore and from around the warming hummocks of grass and sedge, and the first touch of thaw came to the marsh. Life began to move back into the swale. Spotted salamanders migrated overland as soon as spring rain and mists enlivened the dark nights and in a matter of days completed their breeding, leaving great round jelly-like egg masses on submerged vegetation and branches. Every spring they seek seasonal, temporary pools, such as those in the swale, to avoid the greater predation that would threaten the eggs and larval salamanders in permanent bodies of water where fish could get at them. The timing of the development and hatching of the eggs and of the metamorphosis of the gill-breathing salamander larvae into air-breathing adults is intimately connected with the life of the spring pool itself. Given an average season, the surviving salamanders will depart from their hatchery and take up their terrestrial life just as the water that first sustained them dries up beneath their newly developed feet.

Wood frogs appeared in the swale at almost the same time and were the first frogs to sing. Their song is a series of coarse, quacking calls that are music enough to their own kind, which congregate in great numbers to fulfill their own mating rituals and nurture the development of their tadpoles into land-dwelling frogs. The wood frogs were no sooner heard than the first sharp piping calls of the tiny spring peepers pierced the evening air, first as pioneer individuals anxious to get on with the season, then as duets, quartets, and finally vibrant, night-encompassing choruses. As wood frogs begin to string their great egg masses near the surface of the water, and peepers to deposit their numberless eggs singly in hiding places within the sunken plant growth, the explosion of life that follows emergence is imminent.

Something stirs the spotted turtle. Just as the amphibious invasion of the swale is reaching its height, life moves in her. The angle of the sun, some slight penetration of heat or light to the bottom of the pond, the scent of the first rains washing off the thawing earth and mingling with the swamp water, something rouses her after a winter of darkness, silence, and stillness. Slowly she reaches out with her legs. She works her way up through the darkness of the thick, cold mud, stretches her head forth, and opens her eyes. Dazzling April light fills the water.

The turtle moves through an open, silvery realm. The plant life had died back and over the winter settled to the bottom, where its continued decay would add to the muck and provide nutrients to help sustain the life of the season to come. Half swimming, half crawling, she makes her way through the chill water, over the warming mud, toward the surface. With eyes that have been closed for more than six months, she looks out on a new season. She

Spotted turtle cryptic basking.

threads her way among the long
strands of sedge and shafts of
rushes and sets the claws of her
forefeet into the dense turf at the
base of a tussock sedge. With deep,
steady breaths, her hindlegs out
behind her in the water, her shell
rising and falling with her breathing, the turtle holds fast to her
mooring. She can already feel the
heat moving into her shell at the
water surface. Her head, out in the
air, feels the warmth of the sun.
These first critical breaths of spring-
warmed air bring renewed life.

After a period of breathing and
warming in the top layer of water,
she climbs slowly onto the base of
a hummock of sedge. The dead,
dry vegetation already holds an
agreeable warmth as she rustles in
among the fallen blades of the
plant so that she is partially concealed and settles down with her
black shell at a heat-collecting
angle to the sun. She drowses,
even closes her eyes for a while.
This is a vulnerable time. With
her metabolism reduced to its
finest limit short of death, she has
not lost any appreciable weight
over the long hibernation period,
but the extended time with minimal oxygen has put great stress on
her. It is still early in the season,

and her temperature is dependent on that of her surroundings; only by sunning herself in a sheltered spot can she begin to displace the winter's cold. The same sun that is returning life to the earth itself can bring life back into her.

Chill winds riffle the water and rustle through the dry rushes and sedges in the shallows. The spotted turtle passes her first day basking. As the late afternoon approaches and the sun slips lower in the sky, she turns and slides off the cooling edge of her little island. She sinks slowly to the bottom and digs into a mass of rushes, where she falls into a torpor almost as deep as her hibernation and awaits the return of the sun. Night will come, the temperature will drop sharply, crystals of ice will finger out from the water's edge, but the turtle will be held safely in the water once again.

Spring makes its steady progress, and the sun gradually dispels the lingering cold. The season is on the wing, it seems, just as the birds are, and the cries of the killdeer that broke on the first crystal-melting breaths of March are mingled now with the songs of later-arriving birds, all heralding and welcoming the warmer season.

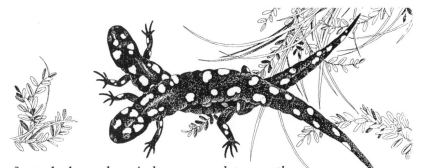

Spotted salamanders, *Ambystoma maculatum,* mating.

No more clouds of pollen drift through the alder thickets; that time passed on as the scattered red maples opened their brilliant flowers to the warming winds of late April and early May.

Beneath the yet leafless canopy of the thickets, brilliant yellow-green ferns uncoil. There is new color in everything, and the near and distant landscapes are enlivened as growth begins. Even the bark on underwater roots glows with intensified blushes of gold and sienna. The gray-green spears of sedge lance another foot into the air.

Though frosts still come on some of the most chill nights, warmth is overtaking the cold. It moves into the earth, air, and water, inspiring ever-increasing life. After sleeping in tangles of roots and sunken grass in a shallow mud depression under eight

inches of water, the spotted turtle awakens once more as morning sunlight filters warmly into the water and touches her shell. Her head extends into the amber glow of sunken leaves in the water. She looks up at the silver surface. For a time she is still. No movement or passing shadow alarms her. Then she backs out of the tight hiding space that she had dug into the previous evening and turns outward toward the open water.

She swims a short half circle and comes to rest at the edge of a mossy island. After cautiously looking out into the world above the water, she climbs up among familiar dried ferns and reedgrass already warm from the morning sun. Her shell, jet black and glistening as she leaves the water, dries quickly. Days like this are common now. She does not have to

wait out the long, dark chill that seemed an extension of winter on so many early spring days and even brought wet snow that disappeared as it touched the surface of the water she slept beneath. If clouds broke enough to let the sun reach her watery world for any part of a day, she would be drawn as if by magic to the surface and out onto the land. When the sun was covered over once more, she would slip back into the water and the sleep of life-suspended and wait for the dream of life-awakened to begin anew.

She is more alert now. As she basks, she cranes her neck and turns her head, watchful of her surroundings. Though she is motionless for long stretches of time, every now and then she shifts her shell in a dialogue with the sun's slow course above her. There is renewed energy in her descent as she slides back into the water.

She comes to rest on the bottom. This time she does not turn toward one of her hiding places but moves her head from side to side and shifts her eyes to investigate the bottom and surface of her pool, as well as the water itself. Warming water temperatures and longer periods of basking have awakened hunger in the spotted turtle, a stirring she has not felt since autumn chilled the waters of the marsh half a year before.

More and more life stirs in the water. Water beetles, crustaceans, snails, and tiny larvae of countless insects move over the muddy bottom and through the submerged plants. Insects are trapped at times on the water surface. Early rains wash earthworms and grubs into water channels and spring pools among the alders and sedge tussocks. Water plants begin to grow, and bright green strands of algae undulate in sunlit patches of the meandering spring flood waters. All of these are sources of food for the spotted turtle as her active season begins in earnest.

Her hunting instincts return. She begins a slow prowling among the sunken branches and the caves under the sedge tussocks. She cocks her head this way and that, extending and retracting her long neck as she explores the countless crevices among the sunken leaves and grass. She stirs up wriggling larvae of mosquitoes as her feet shift through the suspended vegetation in a watery world. They are small, but they are numberless, and her head darts among them

as she begins to eat. Each thrust of her head and snap of her jaws is accompanied by a widening of her throat as she sucks in water. The small prey are drawn to her mouth with the inrush of water, making their capture easier. Her hunting pace quickens now, and she almost dances on the tips of her claws as she moves over the bottom, whirling, reversing herself with quick thrusts of her feet, and lunging forward, following every movement in the water around her.

Suddenly, she freezes in half stride as a dark form shifts in the vegetation. After a moment of complete stillness she slowly arches her neck and almost imperceptibly extends her head toward the spot where a cranefly larva has come to a halt in the midst of its own prowling. The scene rests in a freeze frame for half a minute. The moment the larva starts to shuffle down among sunken sedge blades, the turtle kicks sharply forward, her head darting ahead of the movement in a quick strike that misses but turns the larva back. The second strike, in almost the same instant, is successful. The turtle seizes her prey and quickly draws it back and upward, over her shell at the shoulder, with

the deftness of an angler setting a hook. At the same time, she pushes herself backward by thrusting forward with her front legs. Jerking her head forward with each snap of her jaws, she works her mouth over the body of her prey, increasing her grip, and draws the resisting larva down to where she has set her feet. Once the prey is lowered, she tears at it with her claws, taking her first substantial meal of the season.

More energetic and eager after this, she continues prowling and foraging, taking a fly off the surface, mayfly larvae from the water, rarely surfacing to take a breath. She browses for a time, eating long strands of algae just beneath the surface, then moves underwater to the shaded base of a large sedge tussock. Here she surfaces in a hollow under the thatch that skirts the tussock like a straw hut and looks out at the dazzling sunlight that is still strong on the surface of the water. Nothing moves . . . she is alone in a still and silent world. Her dark shell is nearly invisible beneath the straw in the deep shade of the sedge mound. Not sensing any danger, she makes her way up onto the dense straw mat to sun herself again.

Chapter Two

COURTSHIP & MATING

Perpetually, now, we search and bicker and disagree. The eternal form eludes us — the shape we conceive as ours. Perhaps the old road through the marsh should tell us. We are one of many appearances of the thing called Life; we are not its perfect image, for it has no image except Life, and life is multitudinous and emergent in the stream of time.

—Loren Eiseley

8 May, just past noon. *Sweet, cool, light and variable winds, absolutely cloudless day. After too long an absence, I return to the Digs to look for turtles. May-flowers bloom in profusion on the north-facing slope of the high knoll above Blanding's Marsh. The season has progressed, though the end of April and the beginning of May have been cold, wet, and dark — a miserable stretch of days that would have allowed no sun-ning for the turtles. There have been a few breaks in the clouds during parts of these disappointing days, but they have been brief and widely spaced in time. I don't im-agine that any turtles have been inspired to leave the sheltering water and bask, even in the most select and sheltered spaces. Once again, their season has been held in abeyance.*

Blackflies are biting, making it difficult for me to set down any notes. I hear a green frog calling. I walk along the bank of Bland-ing's Marsh. Redwings and grackles call . . . a song sparrow trills out his beautiful song. The budding brush along the shore and the edge of the woods is alive with fluttering wings and the twittering of tiny birds that take shape for a moment in the maze of branches and then disappear among them. A towhee sings from tree to tree in the distance. I stand in one spot a long while, scanning the water. No turtle appears.

I move on to the Swale and let my eyes drift over the surface, near and to the distance. Spears of reedgrass have appeared every-where. They seem to grow over-night now, and within two weeks will be waist high to me when I step down into the Swale. I watch for any movement among the newly risen grasses that might mark a turtle's underwater progress, and try to look through the surface to search among the dark interstices of vegetation for the edge of a shell or the shift of a turtle's foot. My eyes, ranging over the mes-merizing sunlit surface of the water, suddenly focus on a spotted turtle, jet black, thirty yards or so from shore. Sunlight glints in a point on the dark shape of his head, recently out of the water and still wet. Just beneath the sur-face, the turtle's shell reads in-tensely black. Motionless, he rests on tangles and mats of sunken grasses, which can be the floor of

Song sparrow, *Melospiza melodia,* **on pussy willow,** *Salix discolor.*

his world one moment and the ceiling the next.

I begin a slow progress toward him. I can see the head well enough, with its darker coloration, to know that this is a male. Slowly, I stalk through the water toward the unmoving turtle. My strategy is to get close enough to watch his dive in the clear water, mark his hiding place, and catch him. He takes me by surprise. Suddenly, with midseason alacrity, he wheels on a tight axis, dives, and disappears, leaving no disturbance to trace his flight. With a couple of

Screen of reedgrass, sedge, and blue-flag iris.

sloshing strides I close the distance between us and reach down into the water. The entire underwater realm is deeper and more complex than I had anticipated, with uneven mounds of sedge and grass, fallen trunks and branches of alder, deep pockets of soft mud, and endless masses of previous years' growth providing dark labyrinths through which a turtle could slip in any direction. I grope diligently with both hands. The water has warmed remarkably in a short time, despite days of disappointing chill, and there is no pain in my immersion . . . the season has taken an important turn for the turtles and for anyone who would catch them. My lengthy and resolute search fails to find this turtle. I decide to move on, rather than try to wait out his reemergence, which could take an hour or more. Even then he could elude me, just extending his nostrils to the surface to breathe. At least I know that more spotted turtles are moving into the Swale.

Although the sweetfern is not yet leafing out, its fragrance is heavy among the mingled scents on the air as I walk the dirt road to the Great Marsh. I crumble several dried leaves that have persisted through the wind, rains, and snow of the past seven months and find them still strongly aromatic. Tiny, thin-petalled, deep-magenta flowers, reminiscent of the flowers of the beaked hazelnut that have recently gone by, decorate the sweetfern's stiff twigs. My inspection of the flowers sets clouds of pollen adrift from the male catkins. The environment of these plants, sparse and sun-baked sandy earth, is worlds apart from that of the wetland grasses and sedges, yet it will be a prominent setting in the turtles' season in a month or so, when they move out to nest.

It is hard to pass the cove of the Great Marsh without entering its still and sunlit water. The first lily pads have reached the surface and begun closing in great areas of it. White pendants of leatherleaf flowers arch among their greening leaves. The air grows warmer yet as I turn and walk across the open land; the season grows more benign with the passing of each afternoon hour. Shadbush flowers layer themselves among the branches of taller trees along the edge of the open fields, the grace and sweetness of coming mild days in their abundant delicacy. There is no easier time to enter the landscape, move through it, become part of it.

I pass through the cut in the tree line that divides the sandy fields from the hayfield, walk a short way along the edge of the cleared land, and descend the wooded bank that drops into the alder thicket bordering the Great Swale. In the space of several yards I leave a plane of emerging grass and spreading wild strawberry leaves, cross a carpet of pine needles, and come to a floor of deep sphagnum moss. Goldthread winds around the awakening fern mounds, its dark and shiny leaves setting off the white flowers it trails over the mossy ground. Tiny globes of dwarf ginseng stand above the moist earth. Painted trilliums lift rose-streaked white flowers above their triad of broad green leaves brushed with bronze and maroon. I leave first solid, then spongy earth behind and step into the mud-bordered alder swamps, sidestepping drifts of delicate wood anemone. These are the last of the land flowers I will see as I enter again the water-and-mud realm of alder, sedge, and reedgrass.

The moment I step from the hayfield onto the wooded slope I am joined by mosquitoes, and their numbers increase with every yard I progress into the wetlands. They follow as I head toward the area in which I had found the spotted turtle taking her first sun on a wind-blasted day that seems already to have been part of a separate season. The turning is so recent, despite the flowers now hung in the mild May air and strewn across the warming earth, that there may be other spotted turtles there, basking in the first strong sun of a new year. The water is no longer the icy medium I waded through on my previous expedition, but it is chill enough that my first several steps are taken slowly, as I accustom my feet to the transition from the dry and sun-warmed logging road and sandy fields. Throughout the wetlands, turtles are continuing their ancient dialogue with the sun. The season has not likely advanced enough to inspire their first feeding forays.

I left the hayfield at the same point as on my earlier sojourn, taking the dead crown of a tall red oak as my orientation point. If I retrace my steps, I will be able to see this mark in the landscape even from the sedge marsh

Mayflowers, *Epigaea repens*.

of the Great Swale, beyond the alder swamp. Selecting a route among the alders that looks familiar, I move as best I can along the same circuitous trail that led me to my earlier turtle discovery. I add this to my familiar, often-travelled routes in the marshes, routes I wish it were possible for me to extend and retrace more frequently. I must walk and walk again the same path, be it among the sedges or through the open water or the nesting fields, over different times of day and night between the melting and the freezing, to know the turtles and their season.

I pull aside some twisting alders and push through the interlacing branches of the more slender emergent shrubs that fill the spaces up

Red maple, *Acer rubrum,*
flowering.

to my shoulders. Mosquitoes make
the passage even more difficult. At
length I come upon the seed packet
I left impaled on a small branch.
I had not expected to see it again,
thinking that the wind and rain
would tear it away or that I would
not be able to find such a finite
point in this trackless thicket. I
work my way over to the small
marker, with its photograph of
flowers now fading, and look into
the nest of leaves that had sheltered a turtle three weeks ago.
Many of my turtle findings stay as
fresh images in my mind. When I
return to a site, I expect to find a
turtle there. As swamps and
marshes I have known over my
lifetime have disappeared under

the spread of blacktop and back
yards, many turtles and scenes
have come to exist as image only.
But this wild marsh remains, and
within it lies a fragment of image
and reality that I will come back
to at least one more time, when I return the beautiful turtle to her world.

Now that she is not here to take
my attention, I inspect the turtle's
solarium more closely. The mound
is built up around the sprout clump
of a red maple, rather than an
alder, though the latter is dom-
inant in the surrounding thicket
and has saplings threading up beneath the red maple. Reedgrass
and the dense turf of royal and
cinnamon ferns form the basis of
this island, where the maple has
struggled since its first precarious
roothold. The small tree has had
a difficult time since as a seed it
first drifted onto the thatch of this
wetland island and succeeded in
germinating. It has died back
three times, leaving a dead, branch-
less trunk ten feet high and several inches in diameter each time.
The living sprout reaches slightly
above the dead stems and bears
half a dozen branches, the upper
three with scattered clusters of
bright red and green seeds. Probably it has reached its limit in this

unforgiving environment on a thin
edge between land and water, and
will die back as its predecessors
have. Another sprout will rise up
from the tenacious living roots
and twist its way toward the sun.

Spring floods and summer
drought create an earth-and-water
interchange here, so that the alder
thicket and surrounding sedge
meadow become neither pond nor
woodland, and a wetland is maintained in the ebb and flow of two
extremes. And here the spotted
turtles, neither terrestrial nor
wholly aquatic, find a niche in the
play of the seasons.

I move off among the alders
and cover no more than six yards
when I hear what has to be the
sound of a turtle dropping into
the water. Struggling clumsily
through a channel of mud and
water, I press forward against restraining branches, keying in on
the location of the sound, and ar-
rive in time to see the edge of a
spotted turtle's shell disappearing
into the muck under a tangle of
tree roots. I pull the turtle out of
his hiding place and hold him up
to the sun. Before I could see him,
he had seen me from his occult
sunning spot on a red-maple island
similar to the one on which I

found the female. Their proximity is a convenient arrangement with the mating season only a few warm days away—mating time generally follows hibernation by no more than a month. There is no bonding among turtles. Each goes his or her own way in all aspects of life, save the moment of mating. I believe this male has passed the winter beneath the mound he was basking on. Most turtles would have a more difficult search for a mate than the prospect these two appear to have before them. However, the fact that turtles seek similar situations in which to get through the winter can bring them closer together in spring than is usual later in the season.

I ignore the mosquitoes as best I can and make a rough sketch in my notebook. My hands, one holding the turtle and the notebook in a precarious balance, the other holding my drawing pencil, are particularly vulnerable to the merciless insects. They take full advantage of the fact that I cannot keep interrupting my drawing to swat them. Three layers, each of a different and increasingly noxious repellent, do little to deter the mosquitoes in this environment at this time of year. As the afternoon wears on and twilight comes, they will become impossible.

My drawing completed, I set the turtle on the dark surface of the water. He kicks down through twigs and grasses and is gone. It would seem that the water underlying the expanse of alders and its interspersed red maples would be stagnant, as it is in the smaller Swale, but detectable currents wind here and there among the fern islands and trees. It is evident that the Great Swale is influenced, at least at this time of the year, by watercourses wandering in from the small river several hundred yards distant.

In a shallow arc I work my way back in the direction of the hayfield, taking a bearing off to one side of the dead oak branches I can see in the distance. I ascend the wooded bank with its little landscapes of wildflowers and walk out onto the higher plane of the hayfield, where the day seems to linger. I leave the mosquitoes in the darkening lowland behind me. They will not advance on the open fields until twilight comes.

8 May, 6 PM. *The late afternoon is like a dream . . . May air, wind soughing in the distant pines, gentle and warm on the body. Below the rim of the nesting fields I wade in an ankle-deep, hardbottom cranberry depression, with its spears of sedge rising nearly a foot from the water. Strands of cranberry wind among the new shoots of sedge and the fallen shafts of last year. Like carnelian beads on*

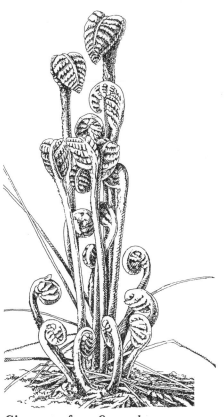

Cinnamon fern, *Osmunda cinnamomea,* **sprouting.**

a lost necklace, enduring berries from last autumn decorate the wine-red strands, most under clear water left by spring rains. Separating the berries are rows of tiny oval leaves, bright green tinged with red. Carpets of bluets spread throughout the sandy fields where the sparse grass and sweetfern have not yet gone to green. There is light across the water and in the water. The air is filled with distant, insistent, plaintive calling . . . the cry of the killdeer. Shallow water, heated by the long day's sun, is warm around my feet. The sun is low in the west. It lies straight across the earth . . . mystical sidelight on spears of sedge and trees alike . . . long, long shadows.

12 May, 12:45 PM. *Return to the Digs to release three spotted turtles. Rain came in the afternoon, with distant thunder . . . the air is cooler now, silver mists have lifted . . . sky soft hazy blue at the zenith. In the east the pale half-moon rides above diffuse clouds, a white moon crisp on its curved outer rim and blurred into the blue of the sky along its median. Killdeer cry in the distance. The air is remarkably still, the sun*

warm on my face. Enough sunlight makes its way through the shimmering white haze in the western quadrant to cast soft shadows on wet sand, beautiful green mosses . . . .

I head to the Great Swale to release the female spotted turtle of 15 April. As soon as I descend to the tangled border where the land reluctantly gives way to water, I am engulfed by mosquitoes, the worst of the season. Every branch and blade of sedge holds a thousand silver droplets, which are showered on me in my passing. Wet, with a chill dropping into its lowlands, light fading, mosquitoes filling the air, the Great Swale is not without its beauty, but I need a good deal of resolution to work my way one more time to the red maple tree and its fading seed packet.

The turtles I will release this evening are quiet in the zippered pockets of my vest as I work my way through the thicket. Black chokeberry is budding up throughout the Great Swale as the related shadbushes of higher ground scatter their final petals and begin to set fruits. The painfully thorned swamp

rose is in delicate leaf. The alder thicket looks different now, even from my last visit. The reaching up and leafing out have made pools and channels all but invisible. The water, in the few places I am able to look into it, is a confusion of darks and flickering lights, interlaced with emergent and submerged branches, arching sedges, and ferns that have unfurled nearly two feet to place their opening fronds throughout the damp air. I place the turtle on her island, and she disappears at once. I hope to meet her again here, or in the nesting fields, during this or some future season.

She has lived here a long time and knows this place well. I counted at least twenty growth rings on one of her plastron plates. Characteristic of older turtles, her shell has become worn, and it was impossible to determine the precise number of the annuli that are formed once each year throughout a turtle's life. After about ten years, with most turtle species, growth rings become indistinct and unable to provide a reliable estimate of age. Some spotted turtles carry clear records of their growing seasons into their twenties, which appears to be the

upper limit of their longevity.

Wading through a fairly well-delineated channel, I leave the alder-and-red-maple zone and enter the open sedge meadow of the Great Swale. Here, at the interface of taller growth and waist-high sedge, hundreds of black chokeberry are in bud. I select a familiar white pine in the distance, on drier ground near the nesting fields, and mark it as the place I will eventually return to land. The spotted turtle in the wild swamp behind me perhaps uses the same tree to orient herself in her seasonal migrations, including her nesting journey. Soaked, chilled, bedevilled in the extreme by insects, I find great happiness in thinking of the turtle in her place. I thread my way along the winding watercourse and look back across the Great Swale to the west, directly into an oversized red-orange sun settling into mists on the horizon, just above the plain of soft-looking tufts of growth and its backdrop ridges of pine and maple. Viewed from a distance, diffused in evening light and mist, it appears a benign landscape that would hold no water at all, let alone a world of turtles.

When I reach the Swale, I wade out into its glowing twilight waters to release two spotted turtles I had caught there several days before. They have kept still in the pockets of my vest but become restless as I take them out into the soft light. Before returning them, a male and a female, to their breeding season, I hold both at the surface a moment. As the female extends her head to look over her surroundings, her throat and chin glow orange in the twilight air above the water. This color may serve as a beacon for males in their water-level searching during the mating season.

Underwater, the male extends his own darker head from his shell. He takes an immediate interest in the female. Despite the reeds and the distance between them, he cannot fail to notice her jet-black shell and glowing yellow spots. He advances, oblivious to my presence (which would not be the case at another time of year), and begins to check her over. He noses at the rear edge of her carapace, around her tail, paws at the

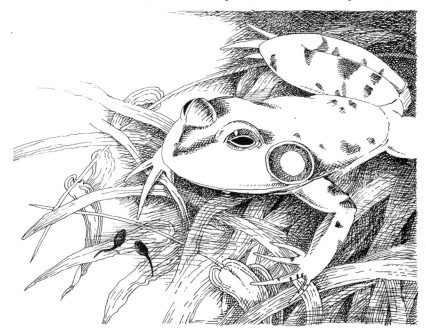

Young bullfrog, *Rana catesbeiana.*

shoulder margin of her shell, and nudges his head against her. The female withdraws into her shell and remains there for several minutes as he makes attentive half circles around her. She comes out suddenly and starts off at once among the underwater tangles. The male follows immediately, and both are soon out of sight. I cannot stay to see if a courtship chase develops; darkness is descending, and the turtles will most likely keep hidden. Whether they

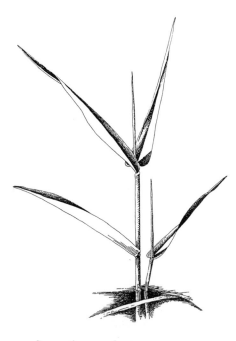

Sprouting reedgrass.

find each other now or in the daylight, or find others of their kind, there will soon be a pairing for each of them.

The male I released had a particularly dark head. There was little orange, even on the underside of his throat, and his lower jaw was nearly black. His eyes were a rich chestnut brown. He contrasted markedly with the female, whose face and throat were radiant pale orange, and whose eyes had a light orange tinge. The differences between a male and a female spotted turtle are more pronounced than those of most species. In addition to darker coloration, the males have decidedly longer and thicker tails, with the cloacal opening farther from the edge of the plastron than is the case with females. As with all reptiles, fertilization in turtles is internal. The male extrudes his penis through his cloaca and into that of the female as they mate. The male spotted turtle also has a concave plastron, which fits over the dome of the female's carapace. The closely related wood turtle has similar distinctions between the sexes. The tail of the male is considerably longer and heavier, and his head and forelegs are larger

than the female's. His plastron is concave and has a deep notch at the posterior margin.

Sexual dimorphism, the difference between male and female, is not as pronounced in snapping turtles, though the male of this species grows larger than the female. In outward appearance the two are quite similar. The cloacal opening of the male is located beyond the margin of his carapace and lies farther back along the length of his tail, whereas the female's is located between the edge of her plastron and the edge of her carapace — but even this distinction can be rather subtle. Among painted turtles the female grows larger, and that difference usually becomes obvious after sexual maturity is attained. The male can be distinguished by the exceptionally long claws on his forefeet, and he also has a long, thick tail with its opening beyond the margin of his carapace. In some species, size differences between the sexes are extreme. Female spiny softshells grow a little more than twice the size of males, attaining a carapace length up to eighteen inches in comparison with the male's eight and a half. Female map turtles grow up to ten and a half inches, while males seldom exceed six.

Coloration, distinctive between male and female spotted turtles, does not vary much between the sexes of most other species. In eastern box turtles, however, the eye of the male has a distinct bright red iris, while that of the female is usually brown or carmine. Another difference in this species is found in the hind claws. Those of the male are thick and strongly curved, in contrast with the female's, which are slender and straighter. These turtles mate on land, and the male has to incline his shell well back on the high dome of the female's carapace, so that his essential grip is taken with his hind claws.

Features distinguishing males from females do not become evident until turtles have attained sexual maturity. This takes from seven to ten years in spotted turtles. Such a long timespan is not uncommon among chelonians; a female Blanding's turtle may not begin to nest until she is fifteen years old. The long time to maturity and the fact that females of this species may not nest every year mean that few new turtles are added to the population in a given

season. But Blanding's turtles are especially long-lived; one has been known to exceed seventy years. With lifespans as long as, or longer than, most aquatic species, they are able to maintain a relatively constant adult population even though their reproductive rate is unusually low. Another turtle that takes a long time to mature is the map turtle. Northern females of this species do not mate until their fourteenth year.

Snapping and painted turtles generally reach maturity in four to six years. There is marked variation in the male painted turtles from north to south; in the southern subspecies they have been known to become sexually mature in one year, while their northern relatives take five or six as a rule, and in some cases seven. The musk turtle also shows variation from north to south, as well as between the sexes. Northern males may mature in their third or fourth year, females in their ninth to eleventh. In a reversal of the usual north-south equation, male musk turtles from southern populations may take longer than those of the North, not maturing until they are from four to seven. The females of the

South may mature earlier than those farther north, at age five to eight. Generally, the turtles of the South reach adulthood faster than those of the North. In some species, size seems to be more important than age in attaining sexual maturity, and those turtles that inhabit regions of long, warm growing seasons may mature several years sooner than their relatives in the cool, shorter-seasoned North.

Once turtles do reach adulthood, their longevity provides them an opportunity to reproduce for many years. Many freshwater species, such as spotted and painted turtles, live into their twenties. Individual turtles may live even longer; one spotted turtle lived for forty-two years in captivity. Some species live thirty to fifty years or more in the wild. Determining the age of a snapping turtle after twenty has proven difficult, but doubtless they exceed this considerably. The eastern box turtle, which has been known to surpass the age of one hundred twenty, is the longest-lived vertebrate in North America.

20 May, 7:30 PM. *Carrying a plastic bag full of water plants and a clump of bluets in a plant*

pot, I slow down along the stretch of road bordering the Swale as I walk out of the Digs. It is mosquito hour here—but it is also the height of the season in this temporary wetland, and I am compelled to slow my pace and have a look. The reedgrass, now waist high, makes the world of the Swale all the more hidden. Few areas of open water are visible from any vantage point. I look in at every passing— each small investigation reveals something. How can this world become so transformed by mid-July, a dry depression choked with reedgrass that is taller than I am?

I have hardly begun to scan the margin of the Swale when I hear intermittent lunging and splashing in the water. Only a turtle could be making such a sound. I listen intently, trying to get a bearing on the disturbance, advancing slowly into the water and searching the openings in the reedgrass. Light is diminishing in the lowland Swale. Maybe a spotted turtle, or even a Blanding's turtle, is feeding at the surface. It sounds as though a turtle is striking at or above the water's surface, perhaps catching insects there or pulling

some from reedgrass blades above the water. At times I hear jaws striking shut. I inch forward, my ears guiding me, until I finally see the water rippling in the chiaroscuro world of the twilight.

In an area of dense emergent growth, a struggle is taking place between two turtles. I cannot yet see either participant in the commotion, but this must be either a mating ritual or two males fighting. I move to within two feet of the rippling and surging in the water, where I can hear turtle shells striking together and scraping over one another, and the sharp snapping of jaws. In a small, almost perfect circle on the water's surface, surrounded by reedgrass strands and shielded from above by an overhanging bower of meadowsweet, two spotted turtles are circling one another, face to face—almost nose to nose—alternately lunging and striking at one another. Their shapes are barely discernible in the water, although they are at, and even breaking, the surface. Their struggle has cleared away all floating and shallow vegetation, leaving them an arena that is just about equal to the area of their two shells combined.

This is certainly not a high-speed courtship chase but some kind of stand-off. The turtles are oblivious to me as I crouch over them, but a sudden movement might startle them away, so I cannot swat at the incessant mosquitoes. The turtles' heads are constantly striking, withdrawing, striking again. They thrust and parry with head and forelimbs, spinning themselves and each other around slowly within the tight circle. One turtle thrusts up and out of the water with the forepart of his carapace and, with a head strike and thrust of his forelegs, backs the other turtle off slightly, but that turtle counters at once with his own surge forward. They lock at times, clinching with strong forelegs and necks, like heavyweight fighters in a hold, then strike out sharply with their jaws, pushing each other back a short distance, all the time rotating slowly, counter-clockwise, within their surprisingly small and narrowly defined ring. They are in fact much like prizefighters. The borders of the arena for their conflict, no more than water, air, and swaying reedgrass, seem to have been roped off to form an invisible and mutually accepted boundary.

I can see the strong salmon color of their forelegs now and make out the dark jaws of two males. Both have large brilliant spots, visible at moments in the dark and splashing water. Their strong, agile forelegs flash brilliantly when they break the surface with a reaching, pawing thrust.

They continue their circling, ever face to face. I try to make out particular patterns of spots on their heads or shells, to see if I might recognize one of them. I think one might be the brilliant male I recently released in Blanding's Marsh, but I cannot be certain. Tirelessly, never pausing, the combatants continue their conflict. The pace is steady, no quarter is given. Throughout the long struggle the two males seem equal to one another in strength and agility. At no point can I detect a sign that either is gaining an upper hand. After nearly half an hour, at eight o'clock, a chorus of eastern gray tree frogs rises up from hidden places throughout the Swale and the alder thicket across the dirt road. Loud, trilling calls fill the evening air. The turtles fight on. There has been no moment of slack between them the

Combatant male spotted turtles.

entire half hour, and as the tree frogs trill off into silence after another quarter of an hour, the sounds of the struggle go on: splashing feet, the hollow grating of shells, and the snap of striking jaws.

The darkening of the Swale grows deeper, mosquitoes become murderous. Several times I come close to abandoning my observation of the tenacious conflict. But any moment might bring some resolution, and I want to bear witness to it. After all this time, neither their energy nor their

Tree swallows, *Iridoprocne bicolor,* **on nesting stump.**

determination abates; neither turtle backs off from the restrictive arena or pauses in his fight. The only biting holds occur when one seizes the fore edge of his adversary's carapace, just to the left or right of his head. The turtle being seized soon breaks this grip, thrusting forward with his own vicious strike and a flurry of his forefeet. It is difficult to follow the contest in failing light and ceaseless struggling, but I do not ever see one get hold of the head or legs of the other with his jaws, and I cannot make out any wounds.

It seems as if the battle will go on after dark. Every once in awhile one turtle slips low on the surface, rushes forward, and rises just upon impact, sending his opponent over backward, his plastron flashing orange and black, forelimbs flailing in the air. Here, I think, might be a decisive blow. Yet the turned turtle invariably rights himself quickly and launches a countersurge, setting both on equal footing in the water once more. Occasionally one rides up onto the other's shell and spins him around with his forelegs. The dull, hollow sound of the two shells grinding together is loud in the stillness of the Swale. But

again, the one who seems to be losing soon counters with his own moves. This would be a difficult match to score. The evenness of the contest is compounded by the fact that at times there is no telling one combatant from the other. I keep a constant eye out for any other turtle in the area, expecting a female to appear and reveal the reason for this conflict, but there doesn't seem to be another turtle around.

Suddenly, one of the males turns and dives. With no turning point that I could detect, one male has become victor, the other vanquished. The diving turtle never stops. He leaves the open arena and pushes frantically through the underwater vegetation, in a wide arc away from his opponent, who with great animation continues to rush about the abandoned arena. He seems to be seeking his rival and is perhaps as surprised by the sudden disappearance as I am.

The fleeing spotted turtle brushes against my submerged pantlegs as he continues his abrupt departure. Off he goes, with no pause, no surfacing to look back, covering many yards in no time at all as he heads for the farther reaches of the Swale. I have never seen a startled turtle, diving and swimming for safety, take such a long, uninterrupted underwater journey. The defeated male is bound away, and the impression is that he will not return.

The victorious spotted turtle keeps to the arena for several minutes, circling and crisscrossing in an agitated search for the foe who is never to reappear. He keeps his search to the surface. After a few minutes, he quiets down and finally pauses, looking around. Only now does he glance up. The two combatant turtles had never taken their eyes off one another and were never aware of me standing over them in the gathering darkness. The turtle cocks his head and regards me. In spite of antagonizing mosquitoes, I keep still. But he reads danger in the unfamiliar form looming above him and dives, disappearing in the reeds and mud. I stand in place a little while, still wondering if I will see a female appear. Some floating bits of reedgrass drift back into the circle of combat, but for the main part it remains distinct even after the struggle has ceased and the surface grown placid once more.

I wade fifteen feet back to the dry land of the logging road. Somewhere in the dark waters that

close behind me, a turtle is hidden for the night in an area he has won for himself. And somewhere within range of that area, I am certain, there is a female of his kind. Over the next several days, the subsequent stages of the breeding cycle will be enacted. The male who was driven away will resume life somewhere else in this three-acre swale. Perhaps he will enter another conflict and emerge victorious. Or he may find an uncontested female and take up the courtship chase. This swale, which will be a dry, dense grassland filled with crickets and grasshoppers within two months, is at this point in the year central to the season of the spotted turtles, too much of which will remain a mystery to me.

March, April, and May are the primary months for turtle courtship and mating. The individual habits of different species and factors of climate and latitude can extend the overall period in North America from February to November. Generally, turtles do not mate until water temperatures have moderated and feeding has begun. Northern species at the Canadian border are still locked in hibernation under great

mantles of ice when males and females of southern relatives are pairing off along the Gulf Coast.

More tolerant of cold water than most species, spotted turtles have been known to breed in early March, with water temperatures at 46°F. and an air temperature of 54°F. Courtship and mating in snapping turtles begin in April, and although most breeding activity has been completed by the end of May, pairs have been observed mating in the months following, into November. Female snappers are among those species that can store live sperm and produce fertile eggs in May or June as a result of a mating late the previous season.

Turtles can take life-sustaining processes to limits that are difficult to imagine. To their extraordinary abilities to go without food (and in the case of tortoises, water) for months, or survive half a year without access to air, can be added a remarkable reproductive resiliency: females of some species can store viable sperm for periods of years. An eastern box turtle or diamondback terrapin, for example, prevented by environmental or other interventions from contact with a male, can lay fertile eggs in a nesting season four years after her last mating. Turtles are unusual in that production of sperm by the male and eggs by the female are not synchronized. Eggs begin to develop in the female in the fall, when sperm production in the male is coming to an end. The sperm cells with which the male fertilizes a female in the spring have been produced the preceding year and kept viable within his body through the winter's hibernation.

Some form of courtship is nearly always employed to lead up to mating in turtles. Although it is most often a peaceful proceeding, courtship and mating at times involve aggression, either in a mating pair, or in a contest between two males over the rights to a female or a little space (including a female, as a rule). Male snapping turtles sometimes stage violent fights, biting and clawing at one another, rolling over in the water, and inflicting serious wounds. Although resisting female snappers can be wounded by males who attempt to subdue and mount them, the courtship is most often nonviolent and can be rather graceful and elaborate. The male and female may approach one another

under water in slow and stealthy grace, stop almost nose to nose, and slowly swing their heads from side to side or thrust their heads out to one side and slowly retract them to a face-to-face position. Once he mounts the female, the male may force his head upon hers, or he may take the skin of her neck in his jaws, as he holds her in place during their underwater mating. For all the prospective power of shearing jaws and cutting claws and the overall strength of these animals, a restraint, if not tenderness, must be the rule in their sexual encounters. I have observed many nesting females, small and large, and they have all looked impressively beautiful and unmarred. Nesting usually follows mating rather closely, and there would not be much healing time for anything deeper than a superficial scratch.

Head-swaying or head-bobbing, gentle or occasionally ferocious head- and neck-biting, and a chase of some sort seem to appear in turtle courtship patterns of widely divergent and geographically separated species and may be retained elements of lovemaking practiced by the ancestral turtles of long ago. Surviving giant tortoises

make use of rhythmic head movements during courtship, as do the smaller tortoises of South America and southern parts of the United States. Wood turtles, which live primarily on land, are also excellent swimmers, and their hibernation and mating take place under three feet or more of water. Before a pair of wood turtles moves on to their final, submerged, copulatory phase, they may engage in a close-up, face-to-face head-swaying on land that lasts up to two hours.

The most terrestrial of the turtles of northeastern North America, the eastern box turtle, will hold his head high in a sort of courtship pose when he approaches a female or heads her off. (The closely related ornate box turtle pulsates his brightly colored throat at this point in his routine.) After holding his head on high, he proceeds with nudging and biting of the female, who in this species can render herself quite unavailable by closing her plastron tightly against her carapace. Should she take a less passive course and flee, the male will follow with vigor, ramming her shell and biting at her head, circling to head her off. When the male attention and insistence, the female mood, and the season are all in order, the female will stop, or come out of her enclosing shell, and mating will proceed. Special cooperation between the partners is required in this species, for the male must take a hold with his hindfeet and elevate his shell vertically at the rear edge of his mate's tortoise-like, high-domed shell, in order to hook his tail around and under hers and maneuver to a point at which intromission can occur. The female may help hold her mate in place, closing her flexible plastron on his hindfeet.

The male's biting and rubbing the head and neck of the female is a recurrent theme in turtle courtship, both in terrestrial and aquatic species. In the small musk turtles, the male lavishes this sort of attention on his prospective mate. In his courting pursuit, he softly nudges the female on the side of her head; if she is receptive and mating proceeds, he arches his long neck and lowers his head, rubbing it gently along the head and neck of the female beneath him. In keeping with their other life habits, these turtles mate at night or in the early morning.

Common musk turtles, *Sternotherus odoratus*, mating.

Stroking with the claws and touching noses take the place of biting and head-rubbing in eastern painted turtles. Following a slow and often lengthy chase by these graceful swimmers, the female turns into the shallows, where the male heads her off and comes at her face to face, extending his forelegs and vibrating his long claws. He slides forward in the water and strokes her head and neck with the backs of his claws as she is suspended in the water before him. He swims backward in front of her, with reverse flips of his broadly webbed back feet, and swims away, then approaches once more to initiate another session of stroking. When the female is ready to receive him, she strokes his outstretched front legs with the bottoms of the much shorter claws on her front feet and sinks to the bottom, where the male mounts her and mating takes place. His elongated claws, which would seem to be a nuisance most of the year,

are helpful here as he maintains a hold on the fore rim of the carapace of the female, who is generally a good bit larger than he is.

Variations on the courtship chase also persist in divergent turtle types in widely varied habitats, from desert sands to ocean depths. The "chase" for tortoises may be more of an ambling walk behind the female by the male. This is quite different from a male green turtle's sweeping pursuit of a female in the extensive open ocean shallows off a nesting beach. In turtle courtship, pursuit is ritual-istic. If the female is not receptive, she will keep moving, lodge herself under something, or swim into an area that is an understood neutral zone, and the male will abandon the chase. If the female is ready to mate and is separated from the male, she will return to him and initiate the chase once more.

Having witnessed the spectacular courtship chase of four-inch spotted turtles in small New England ponds, I can marvel at what it would be like to be transported back in time to witness great Archelon, with his twelve-foot shell, pursuing a mate in the vast, warm shallows of a long-vanished inland sea.

———————— ❧ ————————

As the days pass the season grows even warmer. For a time, fallen red-maple flowers cover the surface of pools and channels . . . these fade and settle into the increasing sediment beneath the water. The flowers have no sooner dropped than brilliant red seeds begin to form. Graceful fronds of royal fern unfurl in delicate light-green lattices, and stout fronds of cinnamon fern thrust and uncoil out of the tawny turf. On every branch and every stem, leaf buds begin to open, spring-green tips that will soon expand and deepen in color, filling in every space of light from the water to the topmost bough, closing out the sky.

Already life trembles and wriggles in the earliest frog and salamander eggs, and pale blue eggs with purplish streaks and spots begin to appear in nests the red-winged blackbirds have woven in sweetgale branches and among the rushes. In time, the spotted turtle wanders outward, beyond the towering ferns, to the edge of the alders and red maples, where a vast sedge meadow lies shimmering in the sun. Here, along the grassy margins of open channels and small pools, she can continue her feeding and sunning. The season of renewing life continues unabated.

Tree swallows wheel in pairs through the open air above the wetland. The lowering sun burnishes a sheen across the curving blades of sedge and glimmers in the thousands of gossamer wings of a mayfly hatch. Swallows drop

and rise, sweep across the level growth of the sedge tussocks, and dip to skim the open water of larger pools, where clouds seem to lie on the land. An amber light glazes the afternoon, radiant on the water surface where the floating leaves of pondweed and waterlilies reflect the sun. The pale orange throat and lower jaw of the spotted turtle glow in the light at a pool's still surface, where her head extends into the warm air. She rests in the shallows, breathing slowly, unblinking and motionless as she surveys the world around her.

Several yards away a dark head emerges wet and glistening at the mouth of one of the many small muskrat channels. A male spotted turtle looks out across the plane. Alert for food and danger, he searches the open surface and the shadow shapes along the grassy margins. The glow on the chin of the female makes him lose heed of prey or predator. Head above the surface, he begins his approach immediately.

The female does not move. She reads the advancing shape. There is a message in the season that neither turtle has responded to since a similar turning of the

previous year. There is no caution in the male, his advance is open. In apparent disregard for everything else in the world around him, he swims toward the female. Suddenly, her head disappears from the surface. She makes a rapid slide along the bottom to deeper water and disappears in the dark tunnels of masses of dead plants. Reaching the spot where she disappeared, the male spins himself to one side and then another, ducks his head and raises

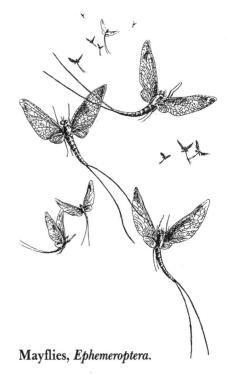

Mayflies, *Ephemeroptera.*

it, presses into shadow and backs out into the light in an animated search. He swirls among the trailing and interwoven strands of sedge and bur-reed, plows among the threadlike stems of pondweed and its long underwater leaves. Almost frantic, he makes short dives, then surfaces again, looking for the shape or color or movement that he will have to pursue.

A jet-black shape shifts in the submarine tangles as the female takes flight. The male fixes his sight on the black edge of her shell with its spots glowing in the water and follows every turn and movement as her legs flash orange in her rapid escape. She takes to the surface, moving at high speed, oblivious to thrashing sounds and dazzling lights of broken water as she races away. Her every turn, dive, and return to the surface is repeated by the following male. His strategy is pure pursuit. She scrambles up onto the mats of reedgrass, rushes across dark mud among the tussocks, and turns back to the water for another dive and long underwater swim. The male follows, losing no ground. His neck is fully extended, his keen eyes entirely fixed on the mate he would have.

The energy and urgency of the season are in both turtles as the high-speed chase continues. When the male makes a sudden surge and nearly overtakes her, the female veers into a dense stand of buttonbush. The underwater roots and stems and crisscrossing stiff branches form an unyielding forest above and below the water, and here the female clambers in an attempt to elude her pursuer. She climbs over thick, rough stems lying at the surface and up among aerial branches, kicking and struggling with great energy. The male follows. She drops back into the water. And here he overtakes her, reaching the back edge of her shell, riding up and over it, straining to grasp the fore edge with his strong claws. She twists away. He overtakes her again, spins her sideways, rides up over her carapace at the shoulder, and bites at her flailing forelegs. She struggles forward. He stays with her and bites at her head and neck. She withdraws into her shell.

Then with a sudden thrust of neck and head and violent kicks of her legs, she breaks the hold of the male and strokes for the surface. His pursuit does not yield. The chase has gone on for nearly

an hour now with neither partner showing any weakness of will or physical strength. He catches up to her and rides her shell again, taking his hold. She grips the rough bark of the buttonbush at the water surface and scrapes under an overhanging tangle, dislodging him, and then dives into the dark underwater passageways among the roots.

He corners her. He turns her from the rear, heads her off at the shoulder, and strikes at her head and legs, vigorously driving her within her shell, her last refuge from his relentless pursuit. She settles to the bottom. He holds fast. The chase is over, and both turtles lie still in the shadows of roots and plants beneath the placid surface. He has locked his front claws onto the fore edge of her shell and hooked his hind claws under the rear edge. His concave plastron fits close to the dome of her carapace. He grows impatient as he awaits her movement and now and then nips at the front edge of her shell, but he cannot reach into the narrow opening between her carapace and plastron, where her withdrawn legs are folded over her deeply hidden head.

The strenuous hour of the courtship chase is followed by a long time of contrasting stillness. Neither turtle surfaces for air. High above, in the slow turning of the afternoon, swallows continue their sweeping, spiralling flights. Insects hatch and move. A great blue heron rises from a leatherleaf island in the great marsh and wings off above the pines to the rookery where young are waiting to be fed. In a hollow tree on a ridge above the marsh, a raccoon quiets her young and waits for nightfall. Green frogs and bull-frogs begin their intermittent afternoon choruses.

The male alternately waits and nips at his mate. In time, the tip of her head appears, her legs and tail extend. The male slides back-ward along the curve of her shell, stretching his forelegs as he main-tains his strong grip. His hindlegs reach downward and under the rear margin of her brilliant spotted carapace, where his hind claws continue to clasp his shell to hers. As he slides down and back, his long, strong tail reaches out and down and curls under hers. Through an hour of stillness, broken only by a slow surfacing for air, the turtles mate.

Buttonbush, *Cephalanthus occidentalis*, and mating spotted turtles.

Chapter Three

NESTING

In the house of beauty, there I wander.
—Navajo poem

26 May, 5:30 PM. *Clearing after rain, warmth returning. The buds of black chokeberry open . . . clusters of these lovely white flowers are layered among the alders and sweetgale. To the Digs, to make my first search of the season for nesting turtles. The past several days have brought heavy rains and temperatures in the 50's; I am certain there was no nesting activity over that period. Crickets already sing the season's advance in the bluestem grass and reindeer moss on the knoll between Blanding's Marsh and the Swale. No pollen drifts from the sweetfern as I brush past it — tiny, fragrant leaves open out of the buds along its stems. Low-bush blueberry suspends pendants of drooping white flowers inches above the bright green beds of moss at the edge of the sand.*

I circle the sandpit at Blanding's Marsh and crisscross the field around it looking for a turtle or any sign of digging. Moving on and retracing my routes of previous seasons, I pass the Swale and walk to the sandpit at the road's sharp turning toward the Great Marsh. I look through this sandpit, check the open, narrow fields and the sweetfern stands all along the dirt road, and then begin a slow circling and crisscrossing of the acres of open sandy ground in the nesting fields. My eyes scan the earth off to the distance for the shape of a turtle's shell, or the glint of sunlight on one, and then minutely examine the ground at my feet for tracks or any disturbance, caused either by turtles or by any of the predators that might be making their own search for nests. I pass through the road's opening in the line of trees and walk the margins of the hayfield, where grass is sparse and the earth is open to the heat of the sun. Off the middle of the hayfield's southern edge a several-acre stand of white pine has been cut out during winter logging. The earth here is bare, as the pines were dense and shaded out any understory except the tall cinnamon ferns along their border. Great heaps of pine tops and branches are strewn over the orange earth, but trails have been left by the logging trucks, and these new areas of bare earth will undoubtedly attract the attention of female turtles as they leave the water and make their overland journeys in search of nesting sites. I add this clear-cut area to the extensive rounds of my nest searches.

Nesting season is near but has not begun: there is not a telltale scratch on the earth. April was more dark and chill than usual — the entire month brought little sun — and the cycle of courtship, mating, and nesting has most likely been held back. On the turning of any dawn or dusk late in May or early in June, the first females will leave the water of ponds,

Black chokeberry, *Aronia melanocarpa.*

Black-crowned night heron,
Nycticorax nycticorax.

marshes, and swales and crawl cautiously out onto the land to look for a place to lay their eggs. Their journey is ancient and perilous.

My own footprints are all that I find as I look over the earth on my way out of the Digs. Hundreds of bright yellow pond-lily buds stand above the still water now, glowing brilliantly in the low, slanting sunlight that strikes them from behind me as I stand with my back to the nesting fields, overlooking the cove of the Great Marsh. I do not wade into the water; for the next three or four weeks I will be concerned with the land. As I approach the Swale, a catbird trills and rolls out a long, complicated song . . . in the distance I hear a white-throated sparrow. A strange cry is uttered from the recesses of the reedgrass: "eeeyawk," a pause, "eyawk," two calls, and then six or seven minutes later three more calls, spaced with definite, equal pauses. Silence, and then another series of five calls. A black-crowned night heron has moved into the Swale; in previous springs here I have not seen or heard one of these birds. Mingled day's-end twitterings and calls of unseen birds in

the darkening brush are pierced by the song of a redwinged blackbird from time to time. A few widely spaced "clunks" from hidden green frogs complete the wonderful tapestry of sound in the stillness of the Swale. The waxing moon is brilliant now, even at 7:15 in the evening, in a sky that has become completely cloudless. Strong winds of the afternoon have died down; all is still . . . not even the reedgrass trembles.

27 May, 7 AM. *44 degrees as I leave for the Digs. The day grows hot rapidly, as the strong sun climbs a cloudless sky and hot winds begin to blow. No sign of nesting, or predation, in my widespread rambles. At 8:30 AM I see three spotted turtles basking in the Swale and observe them from a distance. From mid-May on I give the turtles a wide berth, as I do not want to be a disturbance in the rhythm of their courtship, mating, and nesting. The increasing heat should motivate the females to begin nest searches soon. I leave the fields at 10 AM, having seen no sign of movement on land. The temperature has risen nearly forty degrees in the three hours I have been out here.*

Temperature 80 degrees in the shade as I set out for an evening search at 5:00. On my way to the Digs I see a large female painted turtle who has just crossed the road and is disappearing in tall grass at the edge of a field, far from any water. She is out to nest; the season has begun.

6:17 PM. Four redwinged blackbirds, all males, start up with protesting calls and fly away from a sweetfern stand as I enter the nesting fields and begin my search. The blackbirds were on a hunting foray in this little thicket . . . perhaps they already have little ones to feed back in the marsh.

6:22 PM. A female painted turtle is crossing the path that divides the nesting fields, near the opening to the hayfield. There is a rim of orange, sandy earth around the rear edge of her shell, and her hindlegs and feet are caked with it. She has nested. I pick her up and find that she is very light. These turtles release copious amounts of water as they dig their nests, and the loss of the water and the weight of their eggs leaves them noticeably light as they head back to the marsh. The turtle waves her feet in the air. Her mission fulfilled, she wants only to get back to the sheltering depths. She is a creature accustomed to living underwater in a world beneath the waterlilies, and there is no comfort for her on land. More than a dozen years before, perhaps twenty, as she is a large turtle, her own life began here with an unearthing in autumn or spring. When I set her down, she scrambles off quickly, rustling through dried stalks of last year's bluestem, heading straight for the marsh. I turn and continue in the opposite direction, examining the earth closely. Once her nest is completed, the mother turtle generally makes a beeline for the water. Sometimes I am able to retrace a turtle's steps across the field and discover where she nested, but it's difficult, as turtles conceal their nests extremely well most of the time. This turtle has probably nested within several yards of where I came upon her, but she has done a typically thorough painted-turtle job of camouflaging her nest, and after a diligent search I have not found the site.

6:44 PM. Two painted turtles are nesting quite close to each other along the edge of the hayfield, above the wooded descent to the Great Swale. The earth here has been scraped and scarred, left bare by the removal of several large white pines during the winter's logging. One turtle's shell is tilted back into the earth . . . she is either digging or laying. The other has completed her laying and is in the final stages of covering her nest. I see her tamping the earth hard with her feet and rocking the back edge of her plastron on it. She pivots in a slow circle around the entrance to the nest as she packs the soil. She will then reach out with her hindfeet and draw loose dirt, bits of twigs, leaves, and strands of dry grass from the nearby surface and swirl them over the site of her nest; but I leave before she begins this process, as I do not want to disturb her nesting neighbor. I place a bone-white length of dead pine branch in a line with the nest and a tree stump, as a marker to aid me in locating the nest sites later on.

As I retreat, I almost step on a third painted turtle digging a nest about fifty feet from the other two. Though they nest on rather open ground and I keep an eye out ahead of me as I slowly make my rounds, I sometimes do not see the nesting turtles until I have come close upon them. If something disturbs a painted turtle before she has laid any eggs, she will usually leave the site (even a laboriously completed nest chamber), return to the water, and try to nest another time. Once the turtle has begun to deposit her eggs, however, she will follow through, even though a disturbance comes along. Eggs left in an open nest could never survive, and the female must remain and finish her task even if danger threatens. A mother turtle will occasionally dig a complete hole, then move on to another nesting place and start all over, or return to the water and await another time and place to lay her eggs, even though no outward disturbance seems to have intervened. Turtle embryos become arrested at a very early stage following fertilization and hold there, in the oviducts of the female. The embryos will not resume growing until the eggs have been deposited in the earth. This mechanism allows both the nascent turtles and their mother a margin of weeks during which the most propitious time and place for nesting may be chosen. This option within the overall nesting pattern may be responsible for a clutch or two of eggs escaping the heavy predation to which turtle nests are subject. Field work indicates that ninety percent of turtle nests are lost to predators.

7:15 PM. No more turtles nesting. The moon is with me as I return from another search of the nesting fields. All is absolutely still. And although the shadows are long and the sun is low, the air and earth are as warm as they have been all year at this time of day. At the edge of the hayfield, I find the dark circle of an abandoned nesting hole that shows clearly in the fading light; the turtle who had been starting to nest must have seen me and returned to the water. I regret having disrupted her labor. I will have to go even more slowly and keep a sharper eye out, now that I know the nesting season has begun. The nest hole is completely finished, with a hard-packed oval rim surrounding three quarters of the opening. A chamber reaches back nearly two and a half inches under this rim, its floor approximately two and three-quarters inches beneath the earth's surface. Behind the packed rim is a mound of soft earth the turtle had excavated with alternate scoops of her hindfeet—wetting it as she dug—and placed in a narrow mound five and a half inches long by two and a half inches wide, piled up a little over an inch high. The nest cavity and surrounding mounds are still wet. Many turtles void accessory water from their bladders to soften the soil and make digging easier. The turtle would have packed some of this earth firmly around and over her eggs after depositing them and arranging them with her hindfeet. She would then have filled in the nesting hole with the rest of the dirt.

Moving on, I line up my pine-branch and tree-stump markers and locate the earlier turtle's completed nest. A clamoring of blackbirds rises up from the Great Swale as I kneel in front of the nest and brush aside the grasses with which it has been hidden. The nest is well concealed, and I was wise to have left markers to help me find it. A few clumps of short, sparse grass, sorrel, and barren strawberry grow in the almost bare ground around the nest site. Mosquitoes that have moved up out of the surrounding wetlands engulf me as I crouch over the nest. I do my best to ignore them and concentrate on digging carefully into the nest to verify

that it contains eggs before covering it with a protective screen. I
want to be certain that the turtle
has not false-nested, and filled in
and concealed a nest that contains
no eggs. As is usually the case,
the earth is packed hard over the
egg chamber. I rub aside the dirt
with my fingertips and slowly
work my way down, making shallow scratches with my fingernails.
Small pebbles have been tamped
tightly in with the dirt, but the
mother turtle's conscientious and
arduous compacting would be of
no avail against predators . . . a
skunk could dig out the eggs and
eat them within minutes. A little
less than two inches down I feel
the familiar soft spot as I reach
the chamber that holds the eggs.
I brush this looser dirt aside and
touch the oval surface of the topmost egg. Its white-pink color
glows against the dark wet earth
as I look into my tiny excavation.

Assured that a clutch has indeed
been deposited, I replace the dirt
I have dug away, tamping gently
and trying to make everything as
it was before, even to the final
scraping and camouflaging. I then
place a twelve-by-sixteen-inch rec-
tangle of quarter-inch hardware
cloth over the nest area and drive

Spotted turtle among tussock sedge, royal fern, and alder.

wooden pegs into the ground through the screen, well off to the side of the eggs, to secure it against any predator's digging. Last season I used a double layer of small chicken wire over a trial nest, but the nimble-pawed raiders (skunks, I believe) lined up the holes over the egg chamber and deftly extracted all the eggs without even trying to dig up the screen.

I will try to cover a number of nests of several different species, in an effort to record times of nesting and hatchling emergence, and hatching success. By the middle of August I will have to make daily rounds, checking each nest, even though some of them may not hatch out until next spring. Most painted-turtle hatchlings overwinter in their nests, particularly those of northern populations. But I have found some to emerge as early as the third week in August, and I must be alert to any possibility. At various points around the nesting fields I conceal caches of the heavy wire screens, wooden pegs, and a number of plant pots. The latter I will use to transfer any spotted- or wood-turtle eggs that might be laid in hazardous areas along the hayfield or logging road, where they are apt to be run over by the occasional passing of heavy equipment. Turtles are drawn to nest in sandpits, which in many areas are vulnerable to the ravages of dirt bikes and all-terrain vehicles, and I relocate any nests I can from these maligned places—that would otherwise be valuable ecological niches for a variety of plants and animals. Over recent seasons I have transferred a number of nests and have had a high hatching success; but this year I hope to leave as many nests as I possibly can in place, as that will provide the most reliable field data. Some painted- and snapping-turtle nests I will neither transfer nor cover, but simply observe, to see what their fate might be.

I stand up, brush mosquitoes away, take up my walking stick and move off quickly, lest the mosquitoes regather. Dusk is settling on the long, narrow hayfield. Blackbird racket continues unabated in the darkening alder swamps below. The dry dirt road shines in late-day light before me as I walk out of the Digs, having covered my first nest of the season.

28 May, 7:40 AM. *After searching several nest areas, I find a female spotted turtle wandering near the sweetfern patch in the back corner of the first nesting field. She seems to be heading toward the Great Swale, back to the wetlands. Looking down at her, I see no sign that she has nested . . . there is no rim of dirt on her shell nor any on her legs. The turtle looks familiar. Since she does not seem to be up to nesting, I reach down and pick her up. I check back in my notebook for drawings of spotted-turtle carapaces and their patterns of spots and find that she is familiar indeed. I meet again the turtle I had found cryptic basking on 15 April. This reacquaintance eases my disappointment at not finding a spotted turtle completing her nest, the major objective of a search that began at six this morning. I set her down, and she hurries away across the warming earth toward the surrounding trees, in the direction of the Great Swale. She may have wandered all night, or she may have been on a dawn excursion. Perhaps her journey had nothing to do with nesting.*

It is hard to find spotted turtles nesting here. There are not many of them, and they are scattered and secretive. I have followed some all through the night only to have them abandon their nests after many hours of digging. On some occasions they dig in several places and nest in none. This may help discourage predators who would eat the eggs. It certainly discourages me, who would like to protect them and release hatchlings of this increasingly rare turtle in this wild and suitable habitat. On the fringes of their range, spotted turtles live in small, generally isolated populations. In addition, they have been eradicated from areas of former abundance by the severe depletion of their habitats, a situation that also threatens wood turtles. I make every effort to protect the three to five nests of both these species that I am fortunate enough to discover in a season.

Honking loudly, four Canada geese explode out of the cove of the Great Marsh as I walk into the second nesting field. My quest continues along the edges of the hayfield. White eggshells are scattered on the dark earth a few yards from nesting activity of the previous night. A nest has been dug out, dirt thrown far from the hole . . . the shells of five eaten turtle eggs rest on the open earth.

Dug-up painted-turtle nest.

This will become a familiar sight — the predation has begun.

10 June, 4:30 PM. *Every morning I go out to read the earth; every evening I return to read the earth again. Painted turtles have been nesting, predators have been digging, and I have been scuffing the earth with hand and foot in my explorations; it becomes difficult to distinguish one day's markings from another's, or mine from those of the nighttime prowlers. But rain fell all last night and into this morning — all previous tracks and signs of digging have been washed away, and the ground is a clean slate for me to read.*

When I dig a suspected area and find no nest, I mark the site by filling it back in and stringing a line of small pebbles across it, so that I will not fool myself on a future visit. The skunks are not so considerate, though their diggings are not subtle and I would rarely mistake any of their rootings for a turtle nest. Their successful nest hunts are far from discreet. They are deep craters, with eggshells scattered about. Sixty to seventy nests have

been dug up already, and the ground is littered with shells in some places. These are most likely painted-turtle nests, though some spotted turtles may be numbered among them. I have not found the nests or eggshells of these two species to be reliably distinguishable, except that spotted-turtle eggs may not be buried quite as deep as those of painted turtles. In the case of a dug-up nest, however, even this slight possible distinction is of no use in identification. There is no sign yet of snapping-turtle nesting or predation.

I circle the nesting areas cautiously now, moving surreptitiously along the leafy border among aspens and white pine. Several yards ahead of me a painted turtle is completing the covering of her nest in sandy earth among scattered tufts of bluestem, a couple of yards out from the tree line. I watch her draw the last strands of grass and bits of bark and leaves over her nest. The circle of wet dirt in which she has dug is dark against the surrounding soil but will quickly dry, and the nest will be concealed.

Still, no matter how well it was disguised, every nest but one that I have been observing in the field

has been dug up and its contents consumed. Most often, this happened the first night the eggs were in the earth. Others I have been observing were discovered the second or third night. The predators are relentless and skillful in their egg-taking. In my investigations of raided nests, the only tracks I have recognized are those of skunks, and the only nest robber I have ever witnessed was a late-night skunk. But raccoons are another major nest destroyer, and foxes, minks, weasels, and dogs eat turtle eggs. Farther south, opossums, crows, and snakes are known to dig them up. In some parts of the world, primarily where large river turtles and sea turtles nest, human beings are the major predators of turtle eggs.

Raccoons leave their footprints all around the marsh, and crows wing daily over the fields, but I have found no sign of either one at an unearthed turtle nest here. From what I have been able to observe during my walks in the Digs, predation seems to occur only at night. It has been suggested that after a rainfall a turtle nest is less vulnerable to being discovered; but I have seen nests excavated throughout the summer, in July and August, after many rains have fallen. Hatchlings may be dug out of the nest and eaten at the end of the season, just prior to their own digging out. Those hatchlings who do not emerge from their nests in the fall may also be discovered on the other side of winter, dug out and eaten by predators who locate nests before the hatchlings become active in the spring and make their break for the water. There is no period of positive immunity for the developing turtles. Whether predators are able to see something on the surface of the earth or scent something beneath it, or employ some other unknown detecting method, they are extremely adept at finding turtle eggs. Few nests survive.

The painted turtle departs, scurrying directly back to the marsh. Large snappers will stalk away from a nest with a certain stately confidence, but for other turtles the journey is a scramble. I am sure they have their reasons, though I have never found evidence of predation or attempted predation on nesting females. Accounts do exist of females being attacked, and even eaten, on their nesting journeys, but most of the

time they are not interfered with, perhaps because it is far more difficult to chew up an adult turtle than it is to dig up eggs.

I emerge from my hiding place in the aspens and set to work covering this second nest. This one is quite out in the open, so I do some extra camouflaging, scattering dried grass, leaves, and sand over the shiny wire, taking care that none of this material will affect the temperature of the nest over its lengthy incubation period. I don't think I can fool any natural predators; my disguising is to conceal the nest from any human wanderer who might happen upon it.

I cross the field to an encampment I have made of several pine and oak stumps at the edge of the logging road where it turns to bisect the sandy plane of the nesting fields and, one hundred yards distant, enter the hayfield. After hiding my nest-covering equipment, I take up a perch on one of several old pine stumps from a cutting that took place years before I ever came to this marsh. There are no mosquitoes in the dry, sunlit air. This is a good surveillance point, as it looks over the great expanse of open ground

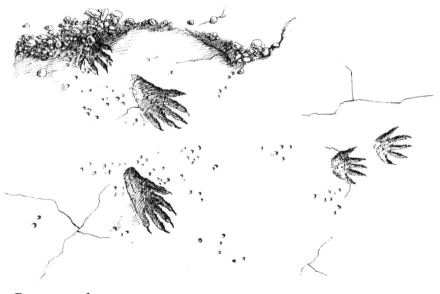

Raccoon tracks.

that will be crossed by many of the turtles coming from the cove of the Great Marsh to nest.

The pair of killdeer who rose up before me, crying plaintively, as I entered the open field quiet down and run along the ground not far from where I sit. These birds nest in the same fields the turtles do, and their piercing calls, flutterings, and wheeling flights are a constant accompaniment to my wanderings, night and day, this time of year. When I am still, they all but run across my shoe-tops. When I make a movement, they cry out sharply, race across the ground, wing up wildly, ca-reen back to earth and flutter and run, crying all the while. Now I am quiet, and the birds are quiet. The hours seem long—they are gen-erous and open and warm in the late afternoons of the lengthening days preceding the solstice. A great blue heron, an emblem of stillness and silence even when in flight, crosses the open expanse of the marsh with slow, rhythmic strokes of its wide wings.

Suddenly, my eyes are caught by light gleaming off the shell of a turtle. With urgency implicit in her movements, a painted turtle heads across the open ground. She stops, with sunlight reflecting bril-liantly on the smooth dome of her carapace, lifts her head high, and looks around. Within seconds she lowers her head and continues her hasty crossing, disappearing in shadows among the tufts of grass. In the distance, I see a momen-tary glint of sunlight on another turtle shell. A glimpse of the size, shape, and general manner of this hurrying female indicates that she, too, is a painted turtle. I stay on my pine stump and keep my vigil for a spotted turtle.

Warm air rises from the earth, which has lain open to the sun since dawn. Mica gleams here and there among the grains of sand and pebbles. The turtles are blessed with these fields and the open spaces along the logging road. Many wild swamps and marshes are ringed with trees and dense overshadowing growth, and a difficult and perilous journey is required for the turtles to find a suitable nesting space, one open to the sun for half a day or more. From what I have seen in the wetlands I have wandered, the availability of nearby nesting habitat seems to have a direct in-fluence on the numbers of turtles living there. The more extensive and more varied the nesting ter-ritory, the more turtles are likely to be found.

The Digs is an extremely rare case of people's disruption of the environment proving beneficial to some plants and animals, particu-larly the turtles. Years ago, trees surrounding the marsh were cut off in logging and cordwood oper-ations. That alone would have opened up some nesting sites. Ordinarily, however, sprouts from the cut-off deciduous trees, and invading grasses and shrubs would quickly cover over the exposed earth. Here, stumps and roots were removed, as well as logs and tops of trees. Then the topsoil itself was scraped off and carried miles away to cover the banks of a highway. Plant succession was pushed back to a stage equivalent to bare rock. It takes decades, if not centuries, for soil to gradually build on such an impoverished, sandy surface and support any abundant or sizable vegetation. The plants slowly colonizing these stripped fields are widely scattered and generally sparse: some mosses, colonies of lichens, bluestem, and sweetfern. A few patches of dur-able flowering plants appear here and there: tiny daisies, birdfoot

Killdeer, *Charadrius vociferus*.

trefoil, hawkweed, and goldenrod. A few pioneer aspens, gray birch, and occasional white pine seedlings creep out from the tree lines, where seeds have found a subsistence in the sand. In the eons before humans and their bulldozers appeared, such natural forces as drought, forest fires started by lightning, hurricanes, floods, and even glaciers caused perturbations that opened up such areas for the plants and animals that require them. American Indians annually burned off extensive areas to enhance their agricultural and other activities, and thereby played a major role in maintaining a richly varied habitat.

The turtles are further blessed by the fact that this entire wonderful ecosystem, with its marsh, small river, beaver dam, stream, swales, open fields, and forest, is well back from any human development or paved road and relatively inaccessible. Endless roads crisscrossing a landscape with everdiminishing wetland habitat are the major hazard a female turtle faces as she heads out on her compelling nesting mission. Nothing in her ancient history prepares her for the danger she faces as she wanders onto a roadway, oblivious to the instantaneous, crushing death that can come from the huge shapes hurtling by. The shell that holds back so much of the menace of the natural world is destroyed in a fraction of a second by the racing wheel of a machine.

Here in the Digs, turtles have a greater choice of nesting sites than they would in most environments, and the three prominent species seem to favor different, distinct zones. Painted turtles generally lay their eggs along tree-lined edges and corners of the field, with no preference I can discern among the east, west, north, and south sides of the trees. In any case, the nests, which are from several feet to several yards out from the trees, receive at least half a day's direct sun. Snapping turtles here, true to their natural history elsewhere, lay their eggs out in the open, usually in pure sand, far from any vegetation. Spotted turtles may occasionally nest in open sand areas, but more often the edges of hayfields or the borders of sparse sandy or dry mossy fields attract them here. In the majority of instances I have observed, they dig within a foot or so of sweetfern or bluestem. This may be a coincidence or may reflect some significant, environmental relationship. It could simply be that the female spotted turtle feels more secure throughout her lengthy nesting process if she is in the vicinity of sheltering vegetation, though one must wonder about those who nest in the open. In turtle activities there seems always to be a pattern and a randomness within the pattern . . . it is not hard to see that an animal's chances of survival over one hundred eighty million years or so would be enhanced by any elements of unpredictability that would preclude its predators' deciphering its habits. It is difficult to say what a turtle seeks when she leaves the water on her maternal mission, what forces and directions guide her. She may wander several hundred yards to nest in a spot that seems identical to one she passed only a few feet from the water's edge.

The scent of sweetfern fills the early evening air. It is a welcome and familiar backdrop to my seasonal wanderings and a particularly distinct feature of nesting time, when I brush among the plants in my searches. The agreeable pungent aroma carries far, especially after a rain, and I often wonder if the wandering turtles are able to detect it. Sweetfern grows in sparsely vegetated, impoverished soil that is usually quite sandy, the type of situation described as a "waste place" in botanical guides. It is also an optimum nesting environment for many species of turtles. If a turtle

travelling the mazes of dense vegetation that often surround her wetland home could detect the characteristic scent of sweetfern, or another indicator plant, and track it to the plant's location, she would have an excellent chance of finding a nest site. It is not certain how sophisticated a sense of smell turtles possess, especially out of the water. In the water many

species are adept at locating food and mates by olfactory means (allowing some to be trapped in baited nets). Tortoises appear capable of doing the same on land. It has been suggested that in some chelonians the sense of smell is superior to that of sight.

What specifically guides turtles on their overland movements — whether to find a nesting site or a

Sweetfern, *Comptonia peregrina.*

new habitat—remains something of a mystery. They have been known to travel more than a mile on such quests. Perhaps these journeys are guided by nothing more than chance, but there always appears to be a direction about them. Turtles seem to be quick to track down and take advantage of new openings in the earth at nesting time, and it may be that a sense of smell plays a role in their finding washed-out, burned-out, or bulldozed areas of land that are far out of sight of their home waterways. A visual clue may guide them; they may read an opening in the skyline, although that would seem unlikely until a turtle had come quite close to a specific place. Whatever may guide her, it is not uncommon for a turtle to show up to nest at a new house site or even a small sandpile that is a comparative pinpoint in the landscape surrounding her wetland. Certainly these small animals have their ways of travelling over an immense and ever-varying earth and finding their place within it, as long as a natural habitat is left to them.

7:10 PM. In the distance, along the edge of a stand of sweetfern in the center of the field I face, a turtle is on the move. I see her in the sun a moment. She is smaller than the turtles I have seen so far, her shell is more abruptly rounded, and the sheen of the sun upon it is somewhat duller. This is quite possibly a spotted turtle. She vanishes along the shadowy margin of the sweetfern. I slowly rise from my long sit and make a wide circle around the field, keeping to the shadows of the tree line. I guess at her location and try to approach, to determine whether she is a spotted turtle and, if possible, to figure out where she will choose to nest. The turtle appears in an open area, wandering toward some clumps of bluestem, and I see that she is indeed a spotted turtle. My excitement is tempered by past experiences, however; I have a long night ahead of me and no assurance that in the end I will have spotted-turtle eggs to hatch.

Different species of turtles have their preferred nesting times. There are always exceptions, but snapping turtles here are primarily true to the species' prevailing habit of laying eggs in the morning, between dawn and noon—though I have seen one finish laying at 7:30 in the evening, and years ago, in a swamp farther south, found one nesting at 10:00 PM. The painted turtles here nest heavily between 3:30 and 7:00 PM, but I have also found them at dawn, at any time throughout the day, and as late as 10:30 at night. All but two spotted turtles I have observed in the Digs have come ashore between 4:30 and 7:00 in the evening and have wandered, dug, and nested through the night, either laying eggs or abandoning completed nest holes in predawn darkness or early morning light. One nesting I observed two years ago was begun at 7:30 in the evening; the turtle finally completed her thorough packing and concealing and left her nest at 10:30 the next morning. Yet late one rainy afternoon last season I came upon two spotted turtles nesting within fifty yards of each other. One finished her nest at 5:30 PM and the other at 8:30 PM, which was more in keeping with reports of their nesting behavior in other parts of their range. Once again I was reminded that one cannot come to hard-and-fast conclusions about the habits of these marsh dwellers.

Moving slowly, keeping to the shadows, and staying well behind her, I follow the turtle for a time. She crosses the open road and moves into the first nesting field. It is difficult to decide whether to follow her or simply to get a feel for where she might be headed and try to find her again later when she may have made a commitment to a nest. She will know the place for her nest when she finds it. She crosses an open area of old wheel ruts, where I saw another spotted turtle dig her nest six years ago, passes an island of sweetfern in the sand where I once saw one nest, and travels without a pause in the direction of a spread of moss and sweetfern in the far corner of the field. Painted turtles nest heavily in this area every year, and every year it is ravaged by skunks. By summer solstice, the shells of nearly one hundred turtle eggs will be scattered over a space of a few square yards. I do not want this turtle's eggs to be numbered among them.

I withdraw, thinking that she will either nest in that area or slip in among the trees and go off to the Great Swale, awaiting another time and place to lay her eggs. I do not want my presence to unsettle her . . . I would do better to try to track her in the dark or in the first light of dawn.

8:12 PM. Long, shrill trills of eastern gray tree frogs break the silence. Darkness closes in. As I circle back to relocate the spotted turtle, I come so close to one before I see her that I run the risk of startling her from her work. Fortunately, I am behind her, and go unnoticed. She has begun to dig—I can barely see the shifting of the back edge of her shell as she uses one hindfoot and then the other to excavate dirt. Even in the pale light there is a soft sheen on her carapace. I can make out the spots on her shell and feel certain she is the same turtle I watched move into the nesting field earlier. In circling the nest areas the past hour I have seen no other turtle. I drop to the ground. She is on a mossy surface, six inches from a clump of bluestem that is growing at the outer edge of the sweetfern. Small white pebbles and patches of sand glow softly on the dark moss. I slide backward on my belly, then turn and crawl into a nearby stand of quaking-aspen saplings, where I can straighten up. The turtle is barely distinguishable now. Mosquitoes have advanced under cover of the spreading darkness and the

coolness taking over the still air . . . they are most intolerable in the hours when day turns to night and when night gives way to day. I am reluctant to leave, but I know the turtle will take many hours, if not the entire night, to complete her nest. In other parts of their range, these turtles sometimes nest in an hour or two, and perhaps there are those in the Digs who adhere to that habit, but I have not seen it. It is also possible that she will dig until dawn and abandon the nest without laying. My best strategy is to make checks during the night and hope to be timely enough to find her finishing the nest. I duck down before I brush the mosquitoes from my face, so the turtle will not see my waving hands. In a crouch I walk away, until I know I am out of sight.

8:40 PM. In a stand of tall pines, dark and distant beyond the open fields, a whip-poor-will starts up. Another sings out his rapid, seemingly endless series of calls from a pine grove. The trilling of tree frogs from the wooded edge of the marsh fades away, and the trilling of those in the alder thickets of the Swale grows louder, as I make my way out of the Digs. I miss the calls of the black-crowned night heron. I have not heard him for four or five days now and assume he has moved on. That strange call had been a constant in my nesting-season sojourns this year, always there to punctuate the midnight silence, the bird chorus of dawn, the stillness of noon, and the nightfall calling of frogs. Mist rises from the channel below the bridge as the air temperature begins to drop sharply.

12:00 AM. On my midnight return to the Digs, moonglow makes my walking easy. In only a few hours, coolness and silence have taken over the night air. Mercifully, there are no mosquitoes. I scan the open areas off to the sides of the logging road with a flashlight beam, looking for any turtle that might have appeared since I walked out or that I might have missed in my previous passing, but see nothing. Nearer the nesting field I turn off the flashlight and move in the darkness at the edge of the trees toward the turtle I hope will still be there. Stars shine in sky spaces among silhouettes of aspen leaves. I make out the pale glow of the pine branch I left lying on the ground to point out the turtle. I draw as

close as I can without turning on the flashlight. This ground is very familiar to me. Countless times I have crisscrossed the acres of earth here, square yard by square yard, and examined it minutely, through the nesting and hatching seasons of seven years.

The clump of bluestem shows in midnight light. I aim my flashlight and turn it on. She is still there, the beam finds her quickly. I watch for less than a quarter of a minute. Her left hindfoot is lifting a pile of earth from a hole that has not been dug very deep yet. Her foot moves very slowly as it reaches out of the hole and adds a measure of dirt to the small mound off to one side of her. I shut off the light. It is disappointing to find she has progressed only this far . . . my hope was to see an egg or two in the nest and be assured that the process would be completed. It is long, hard work, however, and the cooling temperature may have slowed her down. Her style is typical of spotted turtles I have observed, and quite in contrast with that of painted turtles, who sometimes come ashore, scurry to a far corner of the field, dig a nest, lay their eggs, cover and camouflage

the nest, and return to water in little more than an hour.

With no certainty that I will have a spotted-turtle nest to cover this season, I walk away in darkness. As I move out into the field without my light, a pair of killdeer burst up from the earth directly before me, with startled and startling cries. There is only one pair in this field, but their noisy presence gives the impression of a dozen. Before the last turtles have dug their nests, baby killdeer will be racing over the sand — or freezing in place at their parents' command, becoming invisible among stones and grass, while one parent or the other screams piteously and drags a feigned broken wing across the ground. They never tire of playing this trick on me . . . perhaps I should oblige them once and give chase. These birds seem never to sleep. Even when I am distant, silent and still, their calls ring out in the night, at any hour. It is a wild and well-known cry to me and marks my favorite season.

The killdeer quiet down behind me as I walk into the field nearest the marsh and, far from the nesting turtle, turn on my light to search the earth again. Mist off the water lies over the edge of the field and trails away above the dark shapes of the pines. Stars are obscured here. I sweep the nesting areas with my light but see no turtles. There is only that one out here, slowly and deliberately digging her nest in all that space on the cooling earth, under the star-studded sky with its pale moon. I recall the image of her foot, slowly lifting a tiny scoop of earth . . . it could be any time: a million years ago or a million years from now. There is no need for a flashlight as I walk out along the dirt road. The white of moonlit daisies stands out in a near-dark world. In shadows and in moonlight, bluets shine like distant stars.

11 June, 5:30 AM. *Early morning chill lies on the misty trails as I walk back to the turtle's nesting site. She may still be at work. She may have left a completed nest covered with bluestem grass and dried sweetfern leaves. Or she may have abandoned her long labor and left a perfectly excavated nest hole to catch the morning sun. There is some anxiety mixed with my uncertainty, for it is also possible that she finished her nesting and returned to the water, only to have a predawn raider dig up the nest and eat her eggs. The worst sight that could greet me would be dug-up earth and scattered eggshells. I would greatly regret not waiting out the night. But in past times even my midnight presence in the nesting fields seems to have held off predation for one night.*

The hard-packed sand and dirt of the logging trail is wet from fading mists and cool in the shadow of the pines that rise above it on the east side. But the sun has overtopped the ridge enough to slant across the far nesting fields, where white wisps and swirls of mist are dissipating in the rapidly warming air. Forty yards short of my destination I freeze in mid-step. Off to one side, down in a mossy hollow, the rising sun gleams off the mist-wet shell of a nesting spotted turtle. Shafts of grass and small goldenrod stems arch around her in graceful curves, bent by the weight of shimmering dew. Tufts of bluets

Killdeer feigning broken wing.

bend nearly to the ground, their blueness magnified by water beads. In an open mossy section of this damp hollow, the turtle's shell is aslant, backed into the nesting hole she has excavated. Either I missed her in my evening wandering, or she came out under the cover of darkness into this area that I did not check with my light. It is too late to try to pass unnoticed. The turtle holds still. I make a slow circle and move behind young white pines and aspens. Once concealed, I part dew-laden, leafy branches and look back on her. I can barely see her shell, but it seems to shift, and rise and fall slightly. Apparently she has already laid her eggs and now has gone back to covering them.

I creep among the aspens to my lookout point. The first turtle is still on her nest. She has had a long night. Her shell still faces the way it faced ten hours before, but now it rises and falls and tips from one side to the other. Her forelegs maintain the very hold they took when her digging began, but her hindlegs are at work. The sun has warmed and enlivened her. Its first touch upon her shell must have been so welcome and granted her a renewal

of energy for the completion of her great maternal task. I shrink back among the concealing trees to write in my notebook. I take off my sweatshirt. The day is heating up, and even my shirt and swamp vest will be too warm. I creep alternately to the pines to watch the turtle in the mossy hollow and to the aspens to mark the progress of the one I have followed since last evening. I am fortunate they happen to be so near one another. There may even be others nesting, and the wish to be everywhere at once comes over me again.

8:00 AM. The first spotted turtle is in the final stages of filling and covering her nest. She turns her shell in a tight circle as her hindfeet work over the surface above her eggs. I can be less cautious now . . . there will be a nest for me to watch through the season. I wait in the shadows until she completes her process. Her circle widens as she scatters sandy dirt and covering material a foot beyond the packed and hidden entrance to her nest. After a few last scrapings of her feet she turns toward the trees behind her and at 8:25 leaves the nest. She walks several feet into the shade under a canopy of sweetfern. With all four

legs and her head extended, she rests and cools herself. She seems exhausted. The sun has become very hot, and on the open ground her temperature must have risen close to its upper limits. She is breathing rapidly. I slide up to her, pushing myself with elbows and knees as I hold a camera out in front of me. She does not withdraw as I take close-up photographs—perhaps it would be too much effort for her to retreat into her shell. I regret disturbing her after her great work but pick her up so that I can examine her carapace and plastron and make sketches of them in my notebook. I move to the shade of a higher canopy, so that we can both avoid the heat. She does not seem concerned and is patient with my handling. I recognize her as soon as I look at her plastron, which has a distinctive triangular-shaped extra scute. I am, in fact, surprised that I did not recognize her at once—this is the beautiful, large-spotted "Ariadne," a turtle I have found in a corner of the Swale the past three seasons, and only a week ago found in the same place. She has travelled over four hundred yards to nest here. I cannot take long to admire her

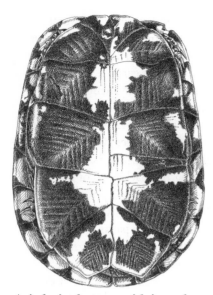

Ariadne's plastron, with irregular abdominal scute.

now, I am anxious to return to the other nesting turtle. And I know Ariadne must be even more anxious to return to her sheltering haunts in the wetlands.

8:44 AM. My timing is fortuitous. The second spotted turtle has just left her completed nest and moved only a few feet in the direction of the thickets that border the Great Swale. When I approach her, this turtle withdraws completely within the unusually high, rounded dome of her carapace, which is also unusually decorated with spots

. . . there are thirty-two on the three front scutes alone. After photographs and sketches, I let her proceed on her way, and I go to the nest she has left behind. It is extremely well hidden . . . I would be hard pressed to discover such a nest, had I not been lucky enough to find the turtle on it. My fingers work carefully into the damp earth. There are times when it is difficult to locate the egg chamber, even when I know where the exact nest entrance lies, because the turtles reach back under a hard shelf of earth after they have backed into a nesting hole and there deposit and arrange their eggs. To dig straight down, or off to the wrong side, would be to miss the eggs. But predators are not fooled by this tactic, as they simply unearth the entire area. Occasionally a snapper's nest, which commonly holds twenty to fifty eggs and is much deeper and larger than those of other freshwater turtles, will be dug into and the eggs not discovered. Early in June of last season I found two snapping-turtle nests that had been raided within a few days of each other. The shells of over sixty eggs were scattered all around the nests, like

clam shells at a low-tide beach. But deep in one nest, exposed to view, lay ten unmolested eggs — and six remained in the other. Whether the predator simply could not eat any more turtle eggs, or whether something frightened it away before it could complete its orgy, I cannot say. These eggs would not survive. Exposed to the air for a season, they would desiccate or possibly overheat, even if they were somehow to escape further detection by the ever-hungry, ever-searching skunks and other prowlers. I carried them home and created a nest for them, and all sixteen hatched the second week of October. On rare occasions I have found an egg or two remaining in a dug-up painted-turtle nest.

My fingertips find their way to the soft earth around the eggs of the spotted turtle and feel their smooth shells. I cover the nest, then turn to the nest of the first turtle, where I find a contrast in style and site selection. The location, in the open in high sandy ground with no surrounding vegetation other than a few strands of bluestem and sparse moss colonies, is more typical of what I have observed in spotted turtles. But for all the time and effort she

took, this turtle concealed her nest more poorly than any I have ever seen in her kind. The "cover" she had dragged in with her hindfeet was piled in a high swirl, like a misplaced bird's nest, directly over the obvious and loosely drawn dirt at the nest entrance. The surrounding surface area was swept clear of any camouflage and featured mother's tiny footprints.

In fairness to this conscientious but possibly unskilled nester, it is hard to say what may work in keeping a nest from detection. The hiding of the nest may be the most important tactic from my perspective, but may be a lesser concern to the turtle in her maternal strategy or to the predator in its detecting. Certainly I have seen the most cleverly disguised nest unceremoniously unearthed and depleted the first night it was wrought. And the fact that all the predation that I have seen appears to have taken place in the dark also makes me wonder about the role of visual concealment in turtle nesting. Many factors may be at work. The marvel is that turtles, confronted with the difficulty of finding a suitable place to nest and beset by such relentless mammalian predation, con-

tinue to survive. I dig into the nest and find the topmost egg barely below the surface. I wonder how this one, with only a quarter of an inch shielding it from the vicissitudes of the season, will survive the summer and how it could ever escape detection by a predator. Yet, whatever extremes the summer brings, and in places where there is no one to fix a sheltering screen in place, there are surely nests exactly like this that will make it and provide a nearby wetland with hatchling spotted turtles.

More than two hundred fifty million years ago a fundamental contribution to the forms of life on earth today was made by animals that preceded the turtles. In their evolution from amphibians they became capable of laying eggs on land, freeing themselves from a dependency on aquatic reproduction and opening a way for their descendants to extend their colonization of the earth's land masses. Amphibian larvae develop from eggs that must be laid in water or wet places in order not to desiccate. The reptilian embryo develops within a complex of fluid-filled membranes. The most important of these is the

amnion, which keeps the embryo from drying out. The development of this membrane made possible the evolution of all higher vertebrates, which are known as amniotes: reptiles, birds, and mammals. As with all amniotes, the embryonic turtle within its liquid medium has a yolk-sac that is rich in proteins and fats, from which it draws nourishment. Surrounding membranes and cavities store the embryo's waste products. A membrane on the inner surface of the eggshell is laced with blood vessels that draw in oxygen and release carbon dioxide through pores in the outer mineral covering, enabling the embryo to breathe.

The heat necessary for incubation comes from the sun, and accordingly the time from laying to hatching varies considerably. Warmer summers tend to accelerate the development of turtle embryos. Depending on how far to the north or south the turtles live and the prevailing weather conditions of a particular summer, eggs of the same species may take less than two months or over three months to hatch. Generally, the timing of turtle nesting and hatching in northeastern North America coincides with the ninety warmest days of the region, which usually fall between the ninth of June and the ninth of September.

Nest temperatures not only influence the rate of development of turtle embryos, but in many species also determine the sex of the hatchlings. In most cases, higher and lower nest temperatures produce females, and an intermediate range produces males. Within the overall requirement that the eggs receive enough heat from the sun to develop and hatch in time, nesting mothers lay their eggs in a variety of situations, and weather conditions provide another variant, so that both males and females are added to the population each season. In some nests, particularly larger ones with greater numbers of eggs (as is the case with snapping turtles), the temperature may vary enough between the top and bottom eggs to produce both sexes from the same clutch. (In some turtles the sex of the embryo is fixed genetically and is independent of incubation temperatures.)

The eggshell, generally somewhat flexible and leathery in aquatic turtles and hard and brittle in tortoises, encloses and protects the embryo in its tiny, pondlike life-support system until it develops into a miniature adult. At this point the baby turtle tears open his eggshell, digs his way to the surface, and emerges into the world, fully capable of taking on life all by himself.

13 June, 7:15 AM. *Geese calling out in the marsh. Several times in my wanderings of recent days a flock of Canada geese has flown across the nesting fields, at times in silence and at times honking wildly. I walk to the far corner of the second nesting field, screened by a stand of red maples and white pines, and creep along the beaver trail that runs beneath them and cuts through the sedge border to a deeper part of the marsh. The beavers have been dragging sapling aspens and red maple through here recently. I wade in the shallow water of an open beaver channel, where I am hidden from the marsh but presented with a broad view of it when I carefully press a few leaves aside. A pair of geese glide majestically into open water. Soon afterward, another pair move in silent grace from behind a great island of leatherleaf. Other pairs appear behind these, until ten geese, all the same size, and I presume adults, are afloat on the clear water. Several glide by me, so close that I see the morning sunlight in their dark eyes. The large birds, which I have not encountered here this time of year in previous seasons, give a new scale to the marsh, making everything around them seem a little smaller. Even great blue herons, which seem giants of the marsh as they descend on their wide wings, seem to disappear into the landscape when they land and fold up those wings and assume their sticklike hunting poses. The geese, by contrast, seem like large, beautifully carved ships as they glide, with no outward motion, in narrow channels among the waterlily pads.*

Redwinged blackbirds disregard me as I watch the geese, and sing at my shoulder. Burreeds sway and jostle in the water at the mouth of the beaver channel. Turtles are moving there. I wait patiently and watch. The geese glide out of sight. Dark shapes of turtle heads appear where the reeds have been disturbed. Several painted turtles raise their shells out of the water at the shoulder and extend their necks and heads, lunging and snapping as high as they can reach up the stalks of bur-reed. I cannot see what it is they pursue — there may be some kind of insect hatch in progress — but I have never seen turtles hunt so actively above the surface of the water or in such proximity to one another.

I withdraw from my hiding place and circle the fields. I go on to explore the two long borders of the narrow hayfield and then approach the clear-cut, which has attracted many painted turtles, and where I found one spotted turtle doing some evening wandering. I round a stand of small, scraggly trees and piled culls left from the winter's logging, and suddenly freeze in my tracks. A good-sized snapping turtle is walking down the hard-packed logging road directly toward me. She stops, lowers herself to the ground, and regards me. I hold still. Slowly, patiently, she looks around, her head high, nose pointing to the sky, but her eyes on the horizon, which includes me. She rises slowly and effortlessly and resumes her stroll. After a few deliberate strides she settles down onto the earth again and remains motion-

less. With some difficulty I maintain my pose, assisted by my walking stick, though my effort to keep perfectly still may be unnecessary, as the turtle takes no apparent notice of me now. She extends her head forward, low to the ground, then arches her long neck and lowers her nose to the earth. She slides forward and paws at the earth with her powerful forefeet.

Unlike the hurrying painted and spotted turtles, she seems to have great patience with being out on land, far from the water. It is hard to imagine a natural force that would interfere with her, and she seems to rest secure in a similar awareness. She turns, eventually, and meanders slowly back up the road, occasionally lowering her head to the earth as if to sniff it, then scratching it, pawing with her front legs — and then moving on. At times she hurls a footful of dirt over her shoulder; the toss sends it flying a yard or two. When she has moved off, I sneak behind her back and circle to a hiding place on a log behind some pines to observe what proves to be very little progress. Following another period of meandering and exploration, the turtle moves out of sight into the shade of the one large

white pine left standing in the area.

At 9:00 AM a painted turtle moves out across the slash to seek a nesting site. The strong smell of pine fills the air in the clear-cut, which is littered with broken branches and slabs of bark. After a wait, I circle out of my hiding place and try to locate the snapping turtle before she sees me. I fail. She has dug into pine needles and turf by a log and is looking right at me when I discover her. I walk away. The habits of a nesting snapping turtle can be more frustrating to follow than those of a spotted turtle. Snappers may wander and dig over a large area of ground for a period of days before committing themselves to a nest. She is well settled, however, into the soft duff and swirls of needles in the heavy shade of the pine and has the look of one who will remain where she is for a long time. I depart, hoping I will be able to return another time this day, or another day, and either find her nesting or discover her nest before the skunks do.

14 June; 7:30 AM. *On my way to follow up on the snapping turtle, I stop to search the sandpits around the wood-turtle area, a* *forested stretch of the brook about a mile downstream from the bridge. A steady drizzle still falls after the violent thunderstorms of late afternoon and early evening yesterday that kept me from my late-day rounds. After a short walk along the dirt road that cuts through sand and gravel pits at the back of a hayfield, I see a wood turtle sitting in the open. The turtle does not seem perturbed by the steady rain or the dark figure I must present as I loom out of the mist and drizzle in my rain jacket. Unblinking, her dark eye with its gold ring regards me. I stand over her, a beautiful female with the color patterns of her dark, sculpted shell brought out by a glaze of rainwater. Then I see swirled patterns in the wet sand her hindfeet rest on, as though she had made a design of waves suitable for a Japanese sand garden. I back away, realizing that this distinct pattern may be the beginning of a nest and regretting that I had approached so closely.*

I go on to the Digs and make my rounds in the falling rain. At first the only wildlife I see is the mosquito, in abundance; then from behind a pile of brush at the edge of one clear-cut I see a snapping turtle, quite likely the one I watched yesterday. Impervious to the rain, she repeats her actions of the day before: wandering, settling, lowering her head to the earth, scraping and tossing dirt. At this point in the season, there is apparently no great urgency for maternal fulfillment. I yield to the rain and mosquitoes and the turtle's gradualism, and depart.

10:30 AM. Back to the wood-turtle area, where there is no sign of the turtle. On the sandy earth where she had rested there is a circular area covered with pebbles that seems to have been smoothed over. Around the perimeter of this circle, about one foot in diameter, is a tidy arrangement of footprints that has not been eroded by the rain, footprints that suggest the turtle has patty-caked her way around a nest, packing down the loose sand. Sadly, this turtle has chosen a site directly in the path of the off-road vehicles that appear over the course of the summer and tear all over the sand flats and steep slopes. Wood turtles move out from trees and thickets bordering the nearby brook to nest in these sandpits, which also provide nesting sites for kingfishers and bank swallows. Unfortunately, the turtles have a predilection for the places torn up by the speeding, heavy-treaded tires.

It is quite likely this nest will be destroyed if it is left in place, so I begin a careful excavation. The wet sand at the surface is soft and loose, but as I come near the egg chamber, I find that it has been packed firmly. Brushing the loosened sand aside, I come upon the topmost egg. It is long, oval, and beautifully translucent pink, about an inch and a half long. Contrasting with the dark wet sand, the egg is the color of a pink freshwater pearl. This egg, the last to have been set in place, lies about two and a half inches below the surface. I lift it out gently, without turning it, and place it in its original position in the material I have scooped from the nest. I brush away more of the remaining sand and uncover a broad, flat layer of six more eggs. Wood-turtle eggs are larger than those of painted or spotted turtles. The nest chamber itself is about four inches wide. I reconstruct this layer of eggs in a large flower pot that I have filled with sand taken from the nest and reposition

Wood-turtle tracks in sand.

the solitary top egg, making every effort to keep the eggs exactly as the mother had placed them, although to rotate them so soon after they had been deposited would probably do no harm. Doubtless they are maneuvered around by the hindfeet that arrange them in the chamber. Turtle eggs are durable, but they are eggs, and I wonder at the deftness of the mothers, particularly the snappers, with their powerful, long-clawed hindfeet, as they go about this ancient practice.

From within a number of hours to several days the developing embryo and its adjacent membrane will rise to the topmost portion of the egg and attach to the inner shell membrane. Following that, any turning of the egg might break this attachment, separating the embryo from its shell and causing it to die. Further along in its maturation, an egg could be turned over, and the young turtle would probably survive and work its way out of the egg upside down at hatching time. Once when I was a boy I found a nest of snapping-turtle eggs that had been washed from a steep, sandy slope by heavy rains and rolled several feet to the bottom of the embankment. I cannot say how long the eggs had lain there, exposed to the elements and potential predators, but they appeared to be in good condition, so I placed them in damp sand and carried them home. It was late in the summer when I found them, and before long the eggs hatched into perfectly healthy turtles, another testament to the durability of the snapping turtle.

I carry my treasure of wood-turtle eggs out with me. I will reconstruct this nest a final time in the sandy hatching area I have established in my back field, where I relocate the nests I find in perilous places.

15 June, 6 AM. *Rains have moved off during the night; a sultry day follows. Sun burns through swirling mist and haze, heat pervades the indirect glare, and the day is quickly on its way to 90-degree temperatures. On a check of a sandy knoll high above the river, I come upon a snapping-turtle nest that has been dug up. A deep crater has been opened in the sand, and at the base of it lies the empty nest chamber, its shape still discrete. The chamber faces east. A dark shadow arches over the floor, which is reached by the day's glare. The nest has the appearance of an Egyptian tomb dug into the*

base of a high, sheer cliff. Torn and twisted shells from more than forty eggs are scattered on a great mound of excavated sand and over the surrounding earth. This nest was plundered in recent hours. Yellow remains of eggs still glisten in ruined shells; slugs and ants have moved in to feed on them. I reach into the chamber and dig with my fingernails. Not one egg was spared.

I steal up to the logging road where I have encountered the snapping turtle, as if by appointment, the past two days and scan the area several times, but do not see her. There are signs that she has been at work, though. Several areas have been roughened up considerably, in patches of a square foot or two. Elsewhere there are scrapings, some no more than a raking of the surface. The earth is extremely hard packed, but her strength and sharp claws enable her to score it with one swipe. I circle the pine beneath which the turtle had dug in two days before and look at the distinct depression left where she had sat for a long time. Finding no new sign of her, I walk down a trail that passes by the pine tree and drops down

Raided snapping turtle's nest.

along a small pond that is part of the wetlands below the beaver dam. American toads fill the air here with their long, drawn-out trilling in the afternoon and into the night.

The snapper has carried her search for a nesting site down this road. I see her pawing at the earth at the edge of the trail, on the slope of an enormous wheel rut. She has nosed more deeply into the earth here and made something of an excavation. When she raises her head to look around, I see that it is heavily caked with dirt. Her broad forelegs are covered as well. She lowers her head and roots and claws at the earth and then lifts her head and crawls up higher on the slope of the wheel rut, anchoring herself with her powerful feet and forelegs. She begins to dig. Her great shell heaves and falls as the alternate thrusts of her hindlegs open up the soil and lift out the first loads of earth. There is no nonchalance about the great turtle now. She proceeds rapidly with her excavation. I have seen snapping turtles abandon deeply dug holes, and I have followed trails where they have dug several trial nests before either nesting at

last or returning to the water to await another day. To the west of this turtle's nesting site acres of open land extend, where the pine forest has been cut down. I shrink back among the trees, make my way to the edge of the hayfield, where I know the snapper cannot see me, and circle the fields again. As I look out from under the cover of the pine trees, I see another snapper on her nest in the center of the second nesting field. Her shell is backed well into the earth, and it is likely that she has begun to deposit eggs. I will cover these two nests with a screen. All other snapping-turtle nests I will not interfere with at all, not even to verify if there are eggs, but will only observe. Last season I covered two nests for data, and found two that hatched successfully in the wild. Those four nests produced over two hundred hatchling snapping turtles (and there may well have been others I had no awareness of), which might constitute an unwelcome disruption to the balance of power in the marsh, despite the fact that even beyond the nest stage predation is heavy and only a small percentage of baby turtles live to adulthood.

I return to my nesting turtle at the edge of the clear-cut. She has been at work over an hour and seems well along in the process. It is likely that she has now completed the flask-shaped chamber deep in the earth and is settling her eggs in place. Her shell lurches, but I keep my distance in tree shadows well behind her and cannot tell exactly what she is up to. Over the course of the next half hour her shell rises from the deep hole as she leaves eggs behind and packs in sand and dirt. She eventually raises herself to the surface, filling and packing with great sweeps of pillarlike hindlegs. Her anchoring forelegs have not yielded their grip at all. The upper layer of sandy earth is kicked, strewn, and packed, then swirled loosely as she prepares to leave the nest. Most snapping turtles do not seem to make much of an effort to conceal their nests. This one typically leaves a depression on the surface, surrounded by shallow mounds of the soil she has disturbed, and a ridge where she has held on with her forelegs that records quite clearly the tail-drag of her departure.

With her shell held high, the turtle turns and stalks down the slope toward the pond. I come out

Snapping turtle nesting.

of hiding and head her off. She seems less perturbed at being intercepted than I expected and settles onto the earth. Sandy soil is still caked on her head—the whole top of her skull is covered—and it sticks to the sides of her nose, around her eyes, and back toward the thick folds of her neck. The ring of dirt around her eyes has turned to dark, wet mud . . . turtles sometimes shed tears as they lay their eggs. Dirt and sand are scattered over her carapace. This turtle has bent her head and shoulders to the task more than any other snapper I have witnessed.

The turtle pivots away from me, raises herself majestically on her legs once more, and slowly starts to stride away. Again I intercept her, and her patience seems to hold as she settles down, plastron to earth, the huge muscles of her forelegs bulging out from under her shell and the thick, muscular folds of her withdrawn neck bunching around her head. She breathes rhythmically and placably and regards me in the manner these turtles maintain when one does not rile them. Were I given to naming snapping turtles, I would call this one "Serena." I do not want to disturb her so recently after she has completed her yearly rendezvous with motherhood, but impressed with the patience (or is it simply exhaustion?) that she seems to possess, I take a small sketchbook out of my vest and make some pencil studies. I wish I had time for a watercolor of her carapace. It has a dull blue luster in the heavy shade of the pine, with a scouring of thin pale scratches and lines. A patina of green, mosslike algae overlays the shield-like form, and the entire effect is of a burnished, ancient bronze from Shang Dynasty China. For nearly an hour I enjoy the company of this wonderful turtle, the relaxed and tolerant time we pass together in contrast to the agitated and violent moments I shared with the great turtles I dragged from their early spring reveries in the water.

The turtle rises once again. My drawing is not complete, but it is time for her to go; I cannot delay her again. To grant her free passage, I shuffle off to one side from where I have been sitting. I believe part of the reason she has been so tolerant of me is that I never stood up and in fact kept myself crouched low to the earth, more or less on a plane with her. Turtles are not reputed to have much of a sense of hearing, but anytime I said anything to her, she would turn and look at me, no matter how softly I spoke. Unhurried and stately, she walks off toward the water. Her offspring, in the form of embryos barely beginning to develop in eggs hidden in the earth, are left in the care of the sun and rain, and the sheltering earth itself . . . there is no way to know what, if any, thought she harbors of them, or of the artist who would try to draw her in a little notebook, as she leaves them all behind.

I wait until she is out of sight, in case it would matter, and begin digging into the nest, scraping and excavating carefully with a trowel I carry for this occasion. Snappers usually lay their eggs in hard-packed areas, and digging with bare fingers would be painful, if possible at all. Once I unearthed forty-five eggs from a nest in the middle of a driveway that was topped with crushed stone. This driveway featured traffic that included earth-moving construction vehicles and was well compacted. I had difficulty digging, even with a trowel; it seemed the turtle had packed the earth back in place with the force of a dumptruck. It does not seem possible that hatchlings could ever have tunneled out of this nest, but I have found that it is not wise to underestimate snapping turtles.

I am getting close to the egg chamber. I set aside the trowel and work with my fingers. Even at this point the earth is dense and abrasive, because of the sand in it. Eventually I feel the soft dirt at the entrance to the egg chamber

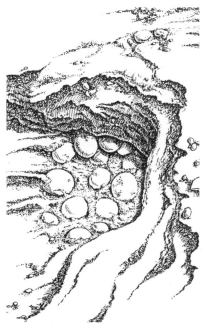

Excavation of a snapping turtle's nest.

and brush it away from the rounded surfaces of the top several eggs. Snapping-turtle eggs are commonly described as small ping-pong balls, and the description is apt. In contrast to the oval, elongate eggs of spotted, painted, and wood turtles, snapper eggs are near-perfect spheres, with a diameter ranging from just under an inch to a little more than an inch and a quarter. They differ somewhat in color from the eggs of the other species, also, having a whiter, more opaque appearance over all, though there is a pinkish tinge at one pole. I fill the nest back in, making myself pack the sand harder than I feel I should, to equal their mother's effect.

Species such as the snapping turtle, which lay more than ten eggs to a clutch, generally lay round eggs, as the spherical unit is the most efficient in terms of the space it takes up, both in the oviducts and in the nest. Those turtles which lay fewer than ten eggs in a clutch tend to produce oval, somewhat elongate eggs. Though they usually lay between twenty and fifty, snapping turtles have been known to lay from eleven to eighty-three eggs. If only one nest in a given year were to escape the heavy destruction wrought by predation and the vagaries of the incubation season, it would probably produce enough surviving hatchlings to maintain the population of its marsh.

20 June, 5:30 PM. *Clouds are high and still, indistinct in the sultry air on the milky horizon. We approach the solstice. Cloud colors float among the waterlilies, which open their first fragrant flowers of the year. The soft rush opens its delicate sprays of flowers from the sides of its arching, pointed shafts. I pass two painted turtles, shells aslant on their nests, and think back to an image of earliest spring: the first gleams of sunlight on the shells of newly emerged turtles basking in straw-colored grass. I will mark the day of solstice with long hours of wandering in the Digs.*

As the hour of solstice draws closer, I walk back to the bridge, having seen no other turtles. There is still light, the light of a hazy sky that has no moon. The brighter stars stand out. Not a breath of air stirs. White mist appears in the hollows and over the water in the lowlands. Dark trees take shape and disappear in shifts of light and mist. Fireflies gleam, glimmer, and are gone, only to reappear here and there — some with staccatos of flickering light, others with long wavering trails of vanishing green, like falling stars caught in slow motion. Fireflies and stars mingle green-blue and blue-white lights on the darkening water. Firefly lights gleam across black tree reflections that lie like ink paintings on the silky surface. When I come back across this bridge at dawn, on my return to the Digs, it will be the first day of summer.

23 June, late evening. *This past week I have seen only painted turtles, and fewer each week. I continue my search for nesting turtles and check back on the nests I have covered at various points in the field: eight painted-turtle nests, two snapping-turtle nests, and two spotted-turtle nests. I also continue to check in on three wood-turtle nests I have been fortunate enough to cover in the sandpits farther down the brook. None of these has been tried; so far the screens have apparently scrambled any clues that predators might recognize.*

The last uncovered painted-turtle nest I have been keeping an eye on has been discovered, two weeks after it was made, and must now be counted among the nearly one hundred fifty nests that have been destroyed. I cannot disregard the open nests and scattered shells I pass in my walking but take heart in the thought that there are nests out here that I am not aware of . . . every autumn and spring I come upon a few hatchlings who have survived the terrible odds against completing their development, emergence, and passage to the water. The only remaining uncovered snapping-turtle nest I have been watching has not been touched since some predator abandoned its digging without reaching any eggs. I have not dug into this, or any other observation nests, for fear of drawing harmful attention to them. I never saw a snapper at work on this one, and cannot be certain, but all signs lead me to believe that eggs lie hidden there, and I wonder if they will make it through the summer.

The season seems to shift . . . no pollen drifts from the reedgrass as I sweep it aside to look in on the Swale. Now that its flowering

White waterlily, *Nymphaea odorata*.

is completed, this grass will gradually draw its open, lacy flower heads into long, narrow seed spikes. The days have become hot and dry, and the water level has dropped markedly. Tadpoles have stubby hindlegs but need more time to turn into land-dwellers than the shrinking water seems to promise. I hope for rain.

In the nesting fields I search the lengthening shadows among bluestem and sweetfern, and walk the long corridor of setting sun where the narrow hayfield runs west, but see no light gleaming from a turtle's shell, no turtle shape in the shadows. Today, or one day soon, the last nesting turtle will return to the water. Though nesting turtles make no sound in their maternal work, these dry

The bridge and channel at night.

fields will somehow seem silent when they have left them for the year.

In my long circling of the fields I see no turtles. When I come next to the marsh, I will return to the water. Except for occasional checks of the nests I have screened, I will not wander the fields again until mid-August, when the hatching begins and draws me back to the land.

At dusk, on my way from the Digs, I come upon a painted turtle travelling the same way I am, along the logging road. I head for the bridge; she heads for the river. She has nested. Although she has probably walked some distance through grass wet with the evening mist, she still carries a ridge of dirt on the back of her shell. I gather her up and carry her along with me. Once across the bridge, I descend the steep bank to a rock ledge at the water line and set the turtle in the channel. She is off at once, sliding deeper beneath the surface as she swims to the buttonbush swamp on the other side. Pale yellow bars on her shell fade out of sight in the dark water; the ripples of her surging descent settle out, and only the sky on the water can be seen with its brighter stars appearing. In saying farewell to her, I am probably saying farewell to all the nesting turtles of the season. At my shoulder, on a thorny branch of swamp rose reaching out of the water, a slit of red shows in a narrow, pointed bud: the first rose of summer.

———————— ❧ ————————

Early June brings a succession of the first hot days of the season. The surface of the water lies serene, glazed by sky glare . . . there is not a breath of air in the afternoon. The spotted turtle hunts in the shallows, among the caverns in the golden strands of reedgrass and the dark shadows at the base of tall new growth. Here the water is alive with tadpoles and salamander larvae, which dart in all directions as she strikes into their midst. With water warming, and fertilized eggs within her, she has become increasingly active.

Without the usual warning of darkening clouds and distant thunder a storm bursts upon the marsh. Out of nowhere, it suddenly flashes across the water. Lily pads turn silver on the churning, lead-gray water. Birds streak out of the roiling sky to seek shelter among the trees. A painted turtle, out to nest, burrows into pine needles close to a log at the edge of the woods. The spotted turtle dives to the bottom and lodges herself in dense growth . . . every living thing settles into solid earth.

Then as suddenly as it had swept down off the mountain, the thunderstorm blows away to the east. Violent winds ease and drop off to a perfect stillness in a matter of seven minutes. Glowering darkness gives way to brightening silver and the sky opens to brilliant sunlight slanting in from the west, back-lighting the retreating storm clouds. Mists rise from the warm, wet earth and hover over the placid water. Points of light gleam from rounded jewels of rain on every floating leaf. A dragonfly wings through the still air and lights on an arching spear of soft rush, releasing a line of silver droplets to scatter dark, widening circles on an open pool beneath it.

Light begins to fill the water. A dusky amber glow spreads among the stalks of rush and sedge and enters dimly into caverns of vegetation suspended over the mud. The spotted turtle backs out of the forest of plant stalks she had wedged herself into, just beneath the surface of the muck, and looks up toward the silvery plane above her. She moves up through the plants, extends her head and neck their full length out of the water, and blinks into the sun.

The air is warm above the water, and warmth rises from the rain-wet earth beyond. The warmest days of the year are beginning, and the turtle senses this in the heat and light around her. The next three months will be the most favorable for baby turtles to develop in their eggs; the time has come for her to nest. She submerges, after a long surveillance of the field of sedges and rank growth before her, and makes her way toward land. It is late afternoon as she leaves the water and crawls up into the wet, soft sphagnum moss in the shadows of the trees. She winds her way over the spongy carpet, around the tall grass hummocks, following dark, vaulted channels

here and there, then pushes through a dense stand of steeplebush and meadowsweet where the land rises slightly. She passes under a nest song sparrows have woven among several upright, close-growing stalks of the meadowsweet. Not far distant, one of the

Royal fern, *Osmunda regalis.*

sparrows sings to celebrate the passing of the storm. It seems to be night in this thicket—only faint light filters down from the bright afternoon above. The turtle crawls along dark corridors on the wet earth, through a bower of red maple and wild apple, and comes out into the light at the edge of the field. Here the tufted carpets of moss are rain bejewelled, and silver beads shimmer on the shiny leaves of running swamp blackberry.

Lengthening shadows from trees along the far edge of the field reach out over the open earth, soaked, but not cooled, by the passing thunderstorm. The turtle moves through moss and grass out onto the sand, where little grows, and rests and warms herself. Her neck is raised and fully extended; her head turns slowly. She is looking, searching. Her pause is short—she lowers her head and thrusts it straight ahead as she crosses the sand. She disappears in shadows among the arching tufts of bluestem. An urgency is implied in her gait, even though her course is a mix of straight lines, doublings back, and sudden circlings off in another direction, interrupted by occasional short pauses when she settles her plas-

tron onto the agreeable earth and rests. She searches with her eyes again, seems to mark a spot, lowers her head, and moves resolutely in its direction. As she emerges from a shadowy forest of sweetfern, another turtle shape approaches. The spotted turtle settles onto the sand and watches the movement. A painted turtle passes close by without a pause, not turning her head away from the straight line of her anxious progress toward the same sheltering marsh the spotted turtle left behind. The painted turtle's carapace carries a crescent of sandy earth on its rear margin, and her hindfeet are covered with dirt. In a short time she disappears in the sweetfern, quickly following an invisible straight line from a hidden nest to the lily-covered water.

The spotted turtle continues her seemingly aimless wandering as tree shadows overtake the field and twilight creeps into the sky, in the gradual overtaking of day by night. In her wandering she occasionally looks out into the darkness, and at times she raises the rear edge of her shell on fully extended hindlegs and lowers her head to the earth. The first eastern gray tree frog trills out. Another

answers. Calls and answers sing back and forth and overlap, becoming a chorus, filling the night air. Mist slides over the field, the world becomes dark and moist. The night air cools quickly, but the earth gives back the heat it collected over the long, pre-solstice day.

After lowering her head and remaining motionless awhile, the spotted turtle begins to scrape at the earth. Her hindfeet kick away surface pebbles, then hook their claws into the surface and scratch it. After several moments of digging, she abandons this spot and restlessly moves on. An hour passes in the darkness. She wanders, rests, and searches. Pale stars appear in the thin mist overhead. The sky whitens in the east above the mist as the moon begins to rise. Among the trilling tree frogs a peep frog calls intermittently, as some of them sing their last songs of the season. Whippoor-wills soon join the night song of the early-June marsh.

Several inches from a bluestem clump, the turtle settles in and begins to dig again. The grass has a pale sheen in the moonlight; the turtle's wet shell is dark. After the clearing and roughing of a two-inch circle on the surface of the

Nesting spotted turtle and skunk.

great field, her digging becomes deliberate. One hindfoot and then the other digs down into the packed earth, dislodges a footful, then lifts it to the surface and reaches out to dump it on a growing mound to either side of her shell. She digs deeper, and even- tually her shell rocks on three legs while one hindfoot reaches to the bottom and extends back under a hard shelf of earth, as she hollows out a chamber for her eggs.

Something moves among the shadows. The turtle freezes in mid- motion. Several yards away, near the tree line, a dark shape shifts furtively over the earth. It turns out of moon shadows, dark black, with a flash of white that catches the light of the moon. Its head is close to the ground, its nose snuffles into the earth. It shifts and sniffs and turns from side to side, doubling back, advancing, crisscrossing, searching every inch of ground. The turtle does not move. The skunk stops and raises its hindquarters even higher into the air as its forepaws tear rapidly into the earth. Five flashes of white shine in the moonscape as the skunk brings the turtle eggs to the surface and eats them quickly. The predator moves on, sniffing to the left and right, back and forth, as it prowls forward. Torn eggshells glisten on the sand near a small dark cave in the earth.

The skunk is out of sight a long while before the turtle moves at all. She abandons her long labor, leaving an empty nesting hole, and heads for the water. She has been digging for hours, and her journey is long, but she does not pause to rest. Even the dark caves under the thickets of meadowsweet and the tunnels through the sedges are threatening. There is no rest for the spotted turtle until she scrambles over the sphagnum moss and slips back into the water. Under a clear reflection of the moon and passing clouds, she slides down among the sheltering strands of bur-reed and sedge in the water.

The next afternoon, as shadows from the aspens grow across the

fields, the spotted turtle wanders again the familiar land beyond her marsh and swale and resumes the search for a space in the earth to which she can entrust her eggs. Shortly after coming ashore, she passes another painted turtle, who is drawing dried leaves and bits of moss over a dark, wet circle on

the earth. The lily-covered marsh is still in full sunlight. Rhythms repeat as the hours pass, and twilight moves across the water. As the first stars become white points in the darkening blue of the sky, the tree frogs call again, and once more peep frogs join in the nightsong. By the time the whip-poor-will whirls out his calls, the turtle has begun to dig. Mist and stars and dark pines decorate the sky above her, seeming to await the moon. She needs no light to dig by. Her shell tilts back into the earth as she opens up a nesting chamber at the outer edge of a fragrant clump of sweetfern. The hours pass. Frogs fall silent; only an occasional whip-poor-will calls. A snowlike light comes over the land . . . the rising moon keeps its appointed rounds, and in the cycle of her own seasons, the turtle keeps hers.

For the seventh early June, following ten seasons among the waterways before she reached breeding age, she has come out onto the open land to fulfill her ancient, maternal role. The digging takes her well into the night. At last the earth is ready to hold her eggs, and she lowers her shell into the nest she has made. Her plastron flexes slightly as she works an egg out from her body and sets it as deep into the earth as she can. Her hindfeet maneuver the egg into position in the nesting chamber. In slow succession a second egg is released, and then a third. Each is shifted into place. She works dirt in among the eggs and packs it firmly but gently. After the fourth egg, she raises her shell, and her feet arrange fifth and sixth eggs atop the others. She lifts herself on three legs, reaches behind her shell with one foot, and draws earth back into the nesting hole. She settles back in to press the dirt around the eggs. The filling is slow. Her shell rocks with the alternating work of her hindfeet and rises and falls as she reaches from surface to depth and back.

The moon slips behind the stand of tall pines at the western edge of the field. Stars brighten in the silent night and then grow faint as light from the returning sun advances from the east. Deer move like shadows as they emerge from the forest to graze along the logging road and the edge of the field. A great blue heron wings in over the tops of the white pines and glides down into the marsh. Killdeer clamor as they run through the grass and return with food for their young, hidden on the ground.

The spotted turtle is still nesting as the sun overtops the high ridge above the marsh and first touches her shell and the earth around her. She continues her filling and packing; the eggs are well behind her now, completely covered with earth. She draws the last of the dirt from the little mound she had made and stamps it down with her hindfeet. Her shell is parallel to the ground now and for the first time turns from its excavating and laying position. She scratches and scrapes at the earth, then draws her bottom shell across it. She lifts herself off the ground on all four feet, then slams the rear edge of her plastron to the ground, turning this way and that, packing down the entrance to the nest hole and the surrounding area. She pulls bleached straws of bluestem and dark leaves of sweetfern from the nearby surface and strews them over the area above the nest. Her hindfeet are covered with yellow-orange earth, and a ridge of the same has not been dislodged from the back end of her shell by her earth moving. Her pressing and tangling of covering material extends beyond the circumference of the nest. Even as she retreats, she continues to tamp and rearrange fallen vegetation more than a foot from the nest site. Then she is finished. There is no pause for reflection, no look back. She returns to the marsh.

Chapter Four

SUMMER

I did not come to believe,
but to listen for light and to breathe.
Being was my belief
as I breathed with more mouths than a tree.
                              —John Carroll

7 July, 11 AM. *Upper 80's, steamy, the air completely still. The swamps are silent now. Choruses of spring-breeding frogs have given way to occasional bursts of the single notes of green frogs and the rhythmic rolls of bullfrogs that call and answer one another from distant marshy recesses in the late afternoons and into the night. The sun has dropped slightly in the sky since solstice, yet reflects blindingly off the sheets of waterlily and watershield pads that have spread out in tangent to form islands framed by black and sky water. Birds are silent, except for the crows, whose raucous calls from deep in the pines break the afternoon stillness from time to time. Phoebes flit from dead trees in the still water to snatch winged insects in the air or take them from the surface of the waterlily pads. The marsh at midday in midsummer. . . . There will be another round of the seasons before the shrill, startled pipings of the killdeer return to awaken the marsh to spring.*

Life spreads out. Vegetation proliferates explosively along the banks and water margins, out into the shallow water, across the surface of the marsh, and in the depths of the water itself. The survivors of spring become more secretive as they continue their lives and growth.

Heat waves dance up into the air from the land along the shore. The vital sun sustains the life of the marsh. It penetrates the barren earth, where there are no shading leaves or grasses, and continues its slow, remote incubation of the turtle eggs. The nests that have escaped the heavy predation of the early days of the nesting season are now subject to only occasional detection and destruction, and inside the eggs the life of the embryonic turtles advances.

Through reedgrass that towers over my head, I walk the dry main channel to the far end of the Swale to see if pools remain anywhere. Drought conditions followed quickly on the heels of spring floods this year and have prevailed since mid-June, first with unrelenting temperatures in the mid-90's and steamy humidity, then with a sudden shift to cool, dry winds and a succession of chill nights that brought record low temperatures to many parts of the Northeast. Today high summer heat returns. Even in summer there is no stability; the plants and animals of the marsh have few days out of an entire year when the conditions of their environment suit them ideally. Nature achieves evenness through a juxtaposition of extremes. The abundant waters of snowmelt and spring rain have been taken up by rampant plant growth and evaporated by early summer sun and

Pickerelweed, *Pontederia cordata.*

wind. There is no standing water here. Tadpoles wriggle in a few wet places remaining under mats of vegetation, their last effort at survival. I wonder if any of them had time to complete the critical transformation into land-dwelling frogs before the Swale dried up this year.

An extensive spread of cranberry vines flowers over carpets of sphagnum moss at the far edge of the Swale. This moss can store great amounts of water and modify the microclimate of some wetland areas, aiding other plants and animals in its own survival of drought. Tall maleberry shrubs and silky dogwood flower on the landward border of the cranberry mat, and, beyond them, where the ground slowly rises, a dense thicket of meadowsweet is in bloom. Out in the Swale, among sedges beyond the cranberries, clumps of blue-flag iris continue the flowering that heralded the turtles' nesting season. Their first buds opened to reflect on water a foot and a half deep. Now their startling blue arches over dry land on three-foot stems. It would be hard for anyone walking with me now to imagine what a magnificent watery environment this was during my wadings of late May. At the time of the turtles' mating, the Swale teemed with frogs, tadpoles, watersnakes, aquatic insects . . . now grasshoppers leap and crickets sing here. There is nothing else but the wind in the reedgrass and a few furtive birds.

Leaving the Swale, which may not harbor turtles again until after next spring's thaw, I walk around the knoll that separates it from Blanding's Marsh. In my passing I check on the painted-turtle nest I covered near the small sandpit. It is intact; nothing seems to have investigated it in the least. All around the covered nest lie bits of eggshells, dry and shrivelled, from other nests. There is water in Blanding's Marsh, backed in from the river and held constant by a beaver dam several hundred yards downstream, below the bridge. The water in this small marsh is from two to twelve inches deep. Tiny white flowers with yellow centers in the leaf axils of winterberry-holly branches reach out from under the red maples along the shore. These in time will provide scarlet berries to accent the subdued landscape of the winter marsh. I wade past yellow flowers lifted above shallow pools by submerged bladderwort. Slender, curving blades of tussock sedge bow gracefully with the passing of breezes, moving like waves on the ocean.

I part the swaying sedges with my walking stick, searching pools hidden among them, and come upon a tiny, yearling snapping turtle, a little over one and a half inches long, basking on a mat of sedges, completely out of the water. I had hoped the recent series of chill nights would prompt some early morning basking. It becomes very difficult to find turtles in the dense growth that proliferates in and around the water of the marsh in summer; I have a better chance of finding them if they come out to take some sun. Moments later I find a second young snapper, this one a little larger and older, about three and a half inches long and two or three years old, also sunning himself completely out of the water. Neither of these turtles moved a muscle as I reached down to pick him up. Once I set them down where I had found them, however, they tunneled immediately into the layers of vegetation and disappeared in the mud beneath. Even snapping turtles this small rarely bask so high and dry. Perhaps they simply couldn't get close enough to the sun after an uncharacteristically cold spell in summer.

Several times, out in the open marsh, large dragonflies have struck and rid me of circling deerflies, winging so close that they brushed me with their rattling, buzzing wings. One eastern blue darner takes a deerfly out of my hair. Here in the open air I am somewhat protected from the painful bites of these insects that make me think the mosquito season was not so bad. A bite on the elbow received on my walk into the marsh itches and stings yet. Sometimes I stand still as these flies wheel around me with their maddening, relentless circling and raise my arm slightly and open my hand. Often they land on my outstretched hand, and if I close it quickly enough, like a human Venus'-flytrap, I can rid myself of

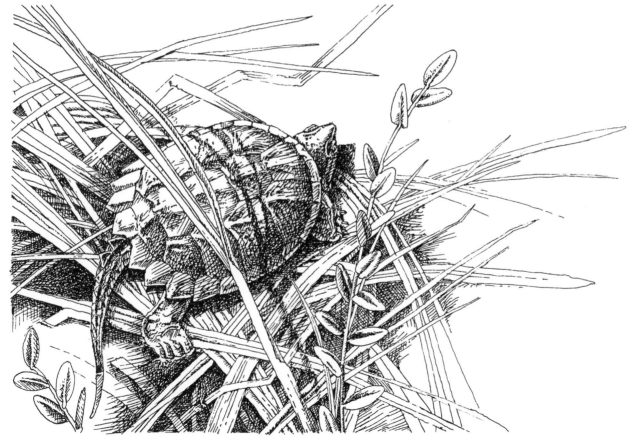

Young snapping turtle basking on mat of reeds.

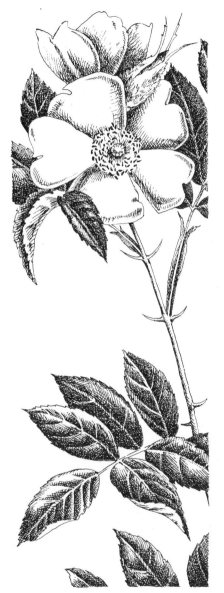

Swamp rose, *Rosa palustris.*

one annoyance.

My slow search of this small marsh is further rewarded by the sight of a spotted turtle sunning himself on a bank of wet mud at the base of a sedge mound. The beautiful pattern of spots along the fore edge of his carapace makes me think of the male who took flight after the lengthy and valiant contest in the Swale during the mating season. But I could not record that turtle and have no way of knowing if this is the same one. Shortly after I sketch the turtle and return him to his marsh, I come upon another, prowling in shallow water off a small channel, his wet carapace almost entirely above the surface. This turtle, another male, is so intent in his hunting that I am able to grab him before he sees me and slips into the muck. This he does immediately after I make a record of his shell and set him back down. It is always impressive to see how quickly these turtles can disappear in an area that would seem to offer no place to hide.

Finding these two spotted turtles elates me. This species is notoriously difficult to find after the nesting season. They become more cryptozooic, or secretive, in their habits, and vegetation proliferates throughout their environment, affording them a life hidden from view. Farther south in their range, where the temporary pools and shallow wetlands they inhabit heat up too much or dry up altogether, spotted turtles dig into the mud under vegetation on pond bottoms or into the damp earth in surrounding woodlands. At times they retreat to muskrat lodges or burrows to escape heat and drought. The turtles are able to survive for months in this dormant state, called *estivation,* which is something of a summer equivalent of hibernation. More than almost any other species, the spotted turtle will often opt for estivation even when suitable habitat seems to be available. In some places, spotted turtles go into estivation late in June and remain in place through the winter, not emerging until the following spring. In times of severe drought, even more aquatic species, as well as those living on land, are able to estivate through an entire summer and emerge with the advent of autumn rains. Some turtles migrate in search of more favorable conditions, however.

Great masses of billowing clouds

have moved in steadily over the past hour and now occlude the sky. It becomes impossible to look into the black water under the waving strands of sedge; its surface has become a mirror. I wade out of Blanding's Marsh, thinking of the turtles I was fortunate enough to find and wondering, as always, what turtles I have missed.

15 July, 9:30 AM. *Hot, still morning. Temperature and humidity rising; it is over 80 degrees already. I begin a long journey to the Great Swale by wading into the buttonbush swamp on the east side of the channel, just below the bridge. I work my way through the dense, woody growth that rises head-high out of water a foot and a half deep, following beaver channels where I can. Closer to the shore the buttonbush merges with nearly impenetrable thickets of winterberry holly, swamp rose, and the ever-present alders. Among these are the familiar tussocks of sedge and reed-grass, with delicate sprays of rattlesnake manna grass. Even these tower above me as I wade the narrow waterways among them. Broad-leaved arrowhead, swamp candles, and swamp milkweed flower throughout the rank, grassy growth, and swamp roses bloom among the alders on hook-thorned stems nearly seven feet tall. The stately royal fern and slender-branched silky dogwood fill in any open spaces above the water with their heavy foliage. As I rest in the deep shadows of an alder thicket just off the main channel, I hear beaver swimming. Four pass by, one pair behind another, in the open, sunlit channel, surging upstream, swirling the water and the leaves of yellow pond lilies.*

I continue my trek and wade past beautiful sprays of cranberry flowering in a mat that spreads over a rock at the water's edge, the one niche this minute plant of the open marsh has found in the rampant paludal growth of the river margins, growth so interwoven and dense that I can barely see my own belt buckle and must set my lead foot down slowly and gingerly, not knowing if it will find water or earth.

Following along this riverine border, I work my way through an alder thicket and emerge on the open sedge meadow of the Great Swale. I follow the narrow channel that winds in from the river; the

Cranberry flower, *Vaccinium macrocarpon.*

Sedge meadow, Great Swale.

narrower tributaries of this channel are muskrat passageways. There is no standing water beneath the sedge this time of year, only a few small pools along the channel's meandering course. I stand at the back edge of the largest of these, to rest and watch for the possible movement of a turtle. A great vista extends before me in the full, hot sun of the open swale, from the delicate, undulating growth of pondweed in the warm shallows at my feet, to distant, columnar, slow-moving thunderheads that tower into the sky just above the hazy horizon. The landscape, with its acres of sedge and surrounding screens of alder flanked by distant ridges of pine, wavers in the heat. Any turtles of this area may well have taken to the shadowy muskrat channels or tunneled into cool mud beneath the sedge. Rose-purple swamp milkweed and rose-pink swamp rose enliven the greens of this shimmering, low-lying landscape. Green frogs, motionless as statuary, are the only living things I see.

Wading across the pond, I begin to follow the channels, which grow more and more narrow. As I round one of the scores of bends in the water's meandering path, I see a spotted turtle's wet shell glistening on a bank of mud and sedge just above the water. I catch the turtle, a female just over three and three-fourths inches in carapace length. As I look her over, I see fresh tooth marks on the fore edge of her carapace and plastron. The black color has been scratched away in long, thin tooth scrapes that fortunately are not very deep. There is no blood, but the wounds look fresh. An image returns to my mind of a spotted turtle's freshly chewed shell lying in a dried-up pond in southern New England many years ago.

Once they have grown beyond a three-inch carapace length, turtles seem generally to be protected by their shell. But the great wariness they exhibit throughout their lives suggests that there is no certitude, even in their remarkable armor of bone. Sometimes this shield is overwhelmed by the teeth or bill of a predator that is big enough, hungry enough, and determined enough. It is not uncommon to find a turtle with chewed edges on his shell and a missing foot or leg. Turtles heal remarkably well and apparently are quite resistant to

infection, as evidenced by their survival of the amputation of a limb or two. More than other species, I have found spotted and wood turtles with such injuries, perhaps because they wander on land more, and come in the way of tooth and claw more than any other turtles except the box turtles. The land-dwelling box turtles are protected by a uniquely designed shell. A single cartilaginous hinge on the plastron of these turtles enables them to draw it tight against the carapace, completely enclosing head, tail, and limbs. The high, rounded shell of the box turtles also serves to prevent an attacker from getting a good chewing grip.

Turtles adjust well to the loss of a foot or even an entire leg. I have caught three-legged turtles on a number of occasions and never noticed any handicap in their escape efforts or their swimming away upon being released. Had I not looked at such turtles closely, I might never have been aware that they were missing a leg. I have heard reliable reports of turtles that have lost both front legs being found in the wild, where they seemed to be faring quite well. A turtle caught in a place of

no escape can only wait it out, within the fortress of his own bones, trusting that it will hold as teeth from the ever-hungry world gnaw away at it. If the shell holds, but a leg is lost, the turtle goes on.

This spotted turtle's wounds seem quite superficial, but as I make a drawing of her shell pattern she extends her neck full

Broad-leaved arrowhead, *Sagittaria latifolia.*

length and pulls her head back, gasping. I cannot guess what might be wrong with her—there is no apparent injury to any part of her body, except for the tooth scrapes. When I have completed my drawing and set her in the water, she tips instantly to one side and floats sideways. With flailing legs she makes a great effort but cannot submerge or even right herself in the water. My first thought is that this is related to her having been chewed on; but it occurs to me that she had more likely developed an illness, could not submerge, and was left open to attack. I have seen captive turtles develop infections, apparently in the lungs, that cause them to float to one side and gasp for breath, but I have never seen it as extreme as this or observed it in a free-living turtle. I rarely find unhealthy turtles in my searches of swamps and marshes—animals of any kind that are not in perfect health are soon overpowered by one predator or another and removed from the scene. A turtle, however, even if quite ill, could survive predation for a time because the structural strength and integrity of its shell could go on protecting a failing body.

Capable of enduring long fasts, a turtle could subsist for weeks or more, even if unable to catch food. Not wishing to leave this spotted turtle to be chewed on by every marsh-dweller that might happen along, I put her in my vest to take her home and keep her in isolation. Perhaps she will recover.

Shortly beyond the point of the spotted-turtle capture, the dwindling waterway enters the realm of another kind of sedge, which grows to my chin. It all reaches to the same level and extends for many square yards. It is as though I look across the water level of some strange, chin-deep pond. Here and there, on this dense, uniform surface of growth, clusters of swamp-milk-weed flowers lie, as though floating on a green sea. The going becomes even more difficult. I feel along with my feet, trying to keep to a muskrat trail that winds through the tall sedge in the direction of the alder border below the hayfield. At one point I slip and fall over backward. The sedge closes over me, and I can barely see the sky. I get up and continue on my way to the alders, where my progress becomes even slower and more strenuous. Any spaces among the twisting, interwoven

alders have become completely filled with summer growth. The pools and channels around hummocks of ferns and trees are dry now; deep, soft mud remains. The spotted turtles I found here in April have either dug in under the alders or moved on to the shallows of the marsh or river. To reach either of these permanent bodies of water would require a journey of several hundred yards for the turtles, something they would easily be equal to.

After wrestling my way through the alder thicket I ascend the incline and walk out onto the hayfield, taking relief in open, level, solid earth. Deciding to keep to dry land for awhile after my arduous crossing of the Great Swale, I make a check of the several nests I have covered with screen in the surrounding nesting fields. None of them has been tampered with. The eggs have been in the ground a month now, and over that time the weather has been unusually hot. At this point, the carapaces of the developing embryos have begun to form and grow, and the embryos have come to look like turtles. How many hidden nests have escaped the heavy predation of spring to harbor eggs in these surrounding fields? In one-inch worlds within shells buried in the earth but touched by the heat of the far-distant sun, tiny hearts continue to beat.

Dismay marks my tour of the first nesting field and its great sandpit. Dirt bikes and all-terrain vehicles have torn through the field and the sandpit. In some favored nesting areas, the earth is deeply scored. The sandpits hold paper targets riddled with bullet holes, and fluorescent fragments of clay targets are scattered over a wide area. I think of asking the landowner if I can post nesting areas against wheeled vehicles, but the last time I did that, two years ago, the signs were shot and run over. Fortunately, people rarely come here, and it is perhaps best for now to leave the matter as it is and not draw attention to this place of solitude and wildness. When I find evidence such as this, however, I am filled with uneasiness. I have seen some wild places absolutely disappear and others become so overrun by human activity that they are ecologically and spiritually meaningless. There is despair in the thought that it may be just a matter of time here.

I take not one of these days for granted, when I can stand among the sedges and look out across the great, untrafficked expanse of this wild marsh, with its turtles swimming and great blue herons winging, and no sounds but the wind in the reedgrass and the piercing cries of the distant hawks.

Since noon, clouds have begun to close over the sky, and now at two in the afternoon it is completely overcast. Trying to put the disturbing image of the nesting field out of my mind, I wade into the sedge shallows of the marsh. Except for the one unfortunate spotted turtle I carry, I have not seen a turtle all day. Now, short, sharp movements in bur-reed and three-way sedge attract my attention. I wade over and reach down among the plants, in water just under a foot deep. In the bottom muck, I feel a turtle shell. To my delight, I pull out a spotted turtle. In addition to the general wanting-to-see-what-I-will-see that draws me to the marsh, my long journey today had the focus of trying to find spotted turtles in the high summer. I have been well rewarded. This turtle, a female, is covered with spots. There are seventy-one on her carapace, not including the

Swamp milkweed, *Asclepias incarnata.*

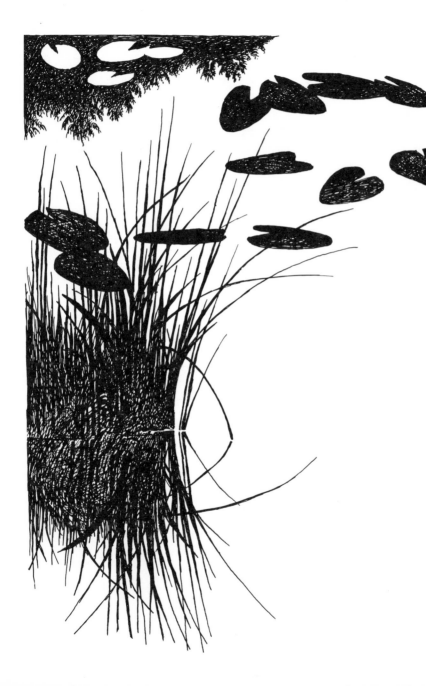

marginals, and thirteen on her head. Even her eyelids carry two spots each. Her life has not been uneventful: a claw is missing from her left forefoot, and she has only a stub of a tail. I stand where I caught her to make my notebook drawing, then set her back down in the water. With a few familiar jostlings in the reeds, she is gone. I leave the marsh and walk out the logging road without looking back on the fresh wheel-ruts in the field.

25 July, 5:45 PM. *Heavy rains in the morning, thunder and lightning, yielding to a day of hazy sun and steamy 80-degree temperatures. For over a week it has rained, heavily at times, turning around the drought conditions that had prevailed for over a month.*

To the Swale, where I find that the water has returned nearly to spring levels. Most years this seasonal wetland would have to await autumn rains, if not winter snows, to be refilled after the summer drying. Immediately I see that green frogs have returned to this favored habitat, and I step down into the water to begin a search for spotted turtles. Crickets sing throughout the Swale, and grasshoppers leap in the forest of grass. These land-dwellers seem quite at home in the growth above the water. Dragonflies rattle among the reeds, and there is a constant flutter of bird wings. Sparrows work through the Swale at the waterline, hopping and fluttering from stem to stem in the sturdy grass. The cover is so dense that these birds either do not see me or feel so confident that they disregard my presence; I could reach out and touch them. I cannot see more than a few feet into the endless screen of grass, which has reached its full summer growth and fills the sky above my head. A song sparrow hops sideways along an alder branch, eating seeds from wind-bent spikes of reedgrass.

After a quarter of an hour of wading, I glimpse several brilliant spots moving in the water off to one side of a channel in the dense growth. The bamboo-like screen of reedgrass serves me well; I catch the turtle before she sees me. Where she has been during the dry spell I cannot say. It is possible that she went into estivation in the drying mud of this very swale, or she may have moved out beyond Blanding's Marsh, to some area along the river, one hundred yards distant. I check the pattern of her shell against sketches in my notebook and discover that she is the turtle I caught at 6:30 one morning, on an early June day last year, just after she had abandoned a completed nesting hole. The site of that capture is about one hundred yards away in the opposite direction of the river, in an open area along the edge of the logging road. A vague picture of this turtle's movements and life begins to take shape in my mind. I hope to find her again and gain another insight into the mystery of where she makes her home. If only I could ask one such turtle her history: the time and place of her hatching, the places she has wandered, where she has nested, where she has passed the long winters of her life . . . I place this one back in the water where she had been cruising, perhaps to take advantage of renewed feeding opportunities provided by the flooding of the Swale. Though the tadpoles and salamander larvae are long gone, having transformed into land-dwelling adults or perished in the drought, the reflooded Swale is alive with insect life.

Turtles move through water and over land and become familiar with wetland and upland areas around them, establishing home ranges within these habitat complexes. One of the more sedentary species is the eastern box turtle. Born into a favorable habitat that suffers no disruption from humans or nature, this turtle may live more than six decades without ever travelling more than two hundred fifty yards from the nest he dug out of as a hatchling. These turtles customarily settle into a daily activity range with a diameter of three hundred fifty to seven hundred fifty feet. Box turtles will on occasion establish two home ranges and a migratory route between them. These may be seasonal, one area being favorable during spring and fall and including a suitable hibernation place, and the other being preferable for the hotter, drier conditions of summer.

Turtles inhabiting deep, stable aquatic environments, such as the painted, redbelly, and softshell turtles, sometimes establish limited home ranges within a lake, deep pond, or quiet river. But even these dwellers of deeper water move around and frequently travel from pond to pond.

Snapping turtles, with their greater size and consequent greater needs for foraging areas, tend to shift their favored zones within a wetland, moving into marshy shallows to feed sometimes, taking to deep water at others. These wanderings are a reflection of the turtle's age and size and may be seasonal. Hatchling snappers are by no means open-water turtles. Barely capable of swimming, they keep to weed-choked shallows, where they can tunnel and hide, stalk their prey, and more or less crawl and climb through the water. During their first few years, all freshwater turtles seek such an environment. Adult snapping turtles, particularly large males, tend to establish fairly fixed home ranges, and they will be found again and again in the same pools. Whether by choice, or by virtue of being forced out, smaller snapping turtles stay clear of water that harbors a large resident. If there is a territorial inclination in turtles, it may exist in this species.

Swales, sedge meadows, marshes, and seasonal streams and pools are all variable over time, even within a season. Species dependent upon such a mosaic of transitional wetland habitats, such as the spotted and bog turtles, must develop flexible, comparatively far-flung home ranges and must also be able to relocate and establish new ones as changes occur. Natural changes occur primarily through plant succession. A succession of different kinds of plants can gradually overtake a shallow marsh, filling it in and in time converting it to dry land. Within the generous lifespan of a spotted or bog turtle, a prime ecological niche can become a shrubby field no longer capable of supporting him. Wood turtles may roam fairly far and wide over the summer months, but they return to the same deeper pools of permanent streams and rivers in autumn, as the time for hibernation draws near, and linger in that area in the spring, through their mating and nesting. These turtles tend to congregate in a favored mating and hibernating territory and sometimes form colonies.

Along with an essentially close-to-home life-style, turtles have a strong sense of homing. Box turtles displaced a mile or two from their home range are able to find their way back, covering a distance that is fifteen to thirty times the radius of the area in which they have lived. Both this species and the wood turtle have been released a little over a mile away in territory that is probably unknown to them and have succeeded in returning home. Turtles released farther away have a tendency to head in the direction of their home base, even though they are not able to find their way back from such a distance.

Aquatic turtles also demonstrate homing ability when moved a mile or so upstream or downstream of their resident body of water or when released a considerable distance away along the shore of a lake. To find their way home in a lake, turtles invariably travel along the shoreline rather than make a direct crossing. Spotted turtles behave similarly in their wetland habitat and have a greater ability to navigate on land, as their season involves more terrestrial wandering than the more aquatic species would voluntarily undertake.

Turtles are not thought to move around much, all things being equal, yet some will set out and cover surprising distances in a few days' time. I have seen turtles make overland migrations in the spring and fall along surprisingly well-delineated routes. On the first hot days of late April or early May, when temperatures are in the 80-degree range, snapping turtles move across the hayfield from the Great Swale to the Great Marsh. Late one afternoon I saw five make this journey in a period of one and a half hours. All of these had a carapace length of eleven or twelve inches, but I have seen three-and-a-half-inch snappers take the same route at other times of the season. There is one diagonal crossing in the nesting fields that snapping, painted, and even occasional spotted turtles follow as though it were a clearly marked road. I have seen even young painted and snapping turtles follow this remarkably straight line, completely out in the open, in broad daylight. One three-inch snapper made this crossing on an afternoon in mid-September, leaving what would seem the ideal habitat of the cove behind, for the essentially dried-up Great Swale, an area he could not possibly see as he set forth. All the turtles making this crossing seem to have a fixed point straight ahead toward which they move unerringly.

The mechanisms behind homing behavior in freshwater turtles are something of a mystery. Their eyesight is good to excellent, and they see in color; visual clues doubtless play an important role in their migrations, water-finding, and homing. Their ability to discriminate among variances in brightness along the horizon probably helps guide turtles in their movements, and they may be assisted by a perception of temperature and humidity gradients, and even a sense of smell. It is also possible that turtles use the sun as a compass in orienting themselves. A range of sensitivities that we cannot even guess at may have enabled turtles to find their way over an enormous span of time in a vast expanse of space.

In the current state of affairs, turtles' journeys all too often take them to the edge of roadways, and it is probably at such junctions that the majority of people-turtle encounters occur. Those inclined to assist a turtle at such a perilous moment are often at a loss as to what to do. The best approach is to get the turtle across the road in the original direction of his or her choosing, if suitable habitat is available within a mile or so and the route to it is not a death trap. If the turtle is wandering between late May and mid-June, it is most likely a female setting out to nest or returning from having nested. In either case, she will not be easily deterred (she may have no choice in the matter), and travelling turtles can in general be assumed to have a compelling reason for being on the road. As far as the turtle knows, the world is still unbounded, an admirable if tragically misplaced outlook. Should the turtle face some land-of-no-return, one can only return him to the nearest suitable habitat and hope his wanderlust diminishes.

In the matter of assisting a large snapping turtle across the road, one can be forgiven for not wanting to become too personally involved. It is wisest to stop or redirect traffic (not the turtle) if possible until the turtle completes the crossing. Where there are speeding vehicles, this may be too hazardous. Sadly, there are times when one can do no more than avoid the snapper and wish her luck.

Turtles of non-threatened species (and perhaps only painted and snapping turtles qualify for this dubious distinction in the Northeast) taken from the wild for observation are best released exactly where they were found. Turtles relocated over great distances may try to get home and set out on a journey that cannot succeed. Some turtles may well be able to relocate and adapt to a new environment given enough time and a habitat in keeping with their needs, but relocation can bring disorientation, and disorientation can be fatal. A further consideration is that a deleterious mixing of gene pools could occur if individuals of the same species are introduced into an isolated, long-established population in another area. Any turtle reintroduced into the wild should have a period of weeks before the onset of cold weather in which to find a safe hibernaculum.

7 August, 6:15 PM. *We move toward autumn; white wood asters and clematis flower at the edge of the logging road, just before the Swale. Winds drift from the north; there is a great break in the humidity, and the temperature is dropping. Quaking-aspen leaves flutter sharply in the transparent air, in dazzling clear light, the first such light in many days.*

I make a tour of the fields, where crickets sing louder every day,

checking the covered nests. They are intact. I imagine the turtles are developing quickly this hot summer. The embryos in the earlier eggs of the season must have reached the point at which they begin involuntary movements. With this first exercise and the increased metabolism it brings, they are preparing for the arduous work of breaking out of their eggshells and digging up from earth, and for the risk-laden journey to water that each must make.

A beautiful small spotted turtle forages among floating grasses at the surface of the main channel in the Swale. I catch her and make a drawing; on one of the shields along the left side of her carapace, several large spots seem to have joined and form a brilliant radiating stripe, something I have never seen before. This is the fourth spotted turtle I have found on five recent evening sojourns to the Swale, where the midsummer rains have brought about a renaissance for these turtles.

12 August, 3 PM. *82 degrees, brilliant cloudless sky, slight winds. The gravel-throated call of a startled kingfisher rattles out along the river as I cross the*

wooden bridge. Cricket song grows more steady in the grassy fields bordering the dirt roads. Meadow rue going to seed along the woodland trail; white wood aster heavily attended by bees . . . purple-headed sneezeweed in flower in the hard-packed and somehow moist earth of the path to Blanding's Marsh.

I come upon a new beaver channel leading into Blanding's Marsh, a well-delineated, worn path that comes straight down from a wooded slope, crosses the grassy trail that borders the marsh, and tunnels through a dense stand of alders, arrow-wood, and silky dogwood. I crouch down and look out through this tunnel, which opens to the wetlands beyond. The beavers have completed this work since I was last here and have cleared a channel that runs thirty yards on a straight line through shallows to the deep pond and river beyond. The water is eight inches deep in this sluiceway, which is a route for transporting saplings they have cut from higher ground for food and construction. I stay here a quarter of an hour, not moving, watching

to see if any turtles might be making use of the beavers' trail in the water. Nothing stirs except a pair of water striders circling on the surface.

I make my way through the beaver tunnel to the edge of the marsh. Despite the heat of the day, the shallow water and the mud in the heavy shade of the alders feels cold. I wade beyond

Shell of young snapping turtle showing toothmarks of predator.

the shadows, where the water has been warmed considerably by the morning sun. If I were only to look across the plane of arching grasses, all curving at the same height several inches above my belt, I would have no idea an aquatic habitat lay at the base of the plants. Yet the water level is constant, and small pools surround each tuft of plants. I might

find spotted turtles in these pools, or even young Blanding's turtles. I make my way laboriously, in a circuitous route, among the hummocks, investigating each small pool I find. Light reflects off the curve of each blade of grass, as though it were a strand of some thin, burnished metal, and makes it difficult to see into the black pools below. I move aside the sprays of grass with sweeps of my walking stick, letting light reach into the water so that I can see to the bottom in some places.

Throughout my long search I find nothing, but even to know there is no turtle here is to know something. However, as I complete my crisscrossing of this small marsh, I find stark evidence of a turtle having been here: at the base of one of the hummocks, near the edge of the shallow water, lies the carapace of a young snapping turtle, upside down. The whitening bones of the spine and broad ribs shine in the sun. I tip the three-inch shell over. The dark upper surface, still edged with mossy, dark green algae, becomes almost invisible as it settles on the mud, attesting to the camouflage that at another time might have saved the turtle's life. But this young snapper encountered a situation in which it needed more than protective coloration. Was it a raccoon? That is always the first predator to come to my mind in a habitat like this; but it could have been a mink, weasel, or fox, or even a skunk that didn't mind getting wet feet to catch its next meal. Any of these hunters of the forest, field, and marsh could have been prowling in this area and caught sight of his movement or heard him rustling in the grass.

Fortress that it can be, a turtle's shell is not inviolable. Young snapping turtles are especially vulnerable because their minimal plastrons afford them no protection, and they haven't the powerful strength and searing jaws of adults with which to mount a successful defense. Even turtles of other species, primarily those with a carapace under three inches in length, are subject to having their bottom shells torn off if they are caught by a strong enough predator.

16 August. *It is the marsh that lives. Its sand and pebbles shift, its waters pulse, its substrate moves. There is breathing in its winds. Its shadows dance with the wind; its plants advance and retreat, replace one another, moving on the passage of time. The marsh takes in light from the sky and reflects light back to the sky . . . its water and earth have an endless dialogue.*

18 August, 3 PM. *Mid 90's. There is heat even in the dense shade of the white pine grove on Pine Point, where I stand to look out over the Great Marsh. The landscape shimmers in hot, humid haze. Unaffected by the oppressive afternoon, waterlilies are still the purest white and retain the crispest form, as they begin to close up for the day. Sultry heat lies in the water and on the land alike. The water level has dropped again in the heat and drought that followed the monsoons of July, and waterlily flowers stand above the surface like lotuses.*

Two sharp, surging splashes in the water break the silence. It could be that a large bass or pickerel has moved into the shallows to feed. The sounds are repeated. They do not have the explosive quality of the warning slap of a beaver's tail, but sound too emphatic to be the leaping of fish. From the shadows of the pines I strain to see through the intense light, the glare from thousands of white-green lily pads that cover the water. The marsh landscape wavers in the heat. Forty yards away, there is an upheaval in the waterlilies at the edge of an island. I begin to think a muskrat will appear. The smooth dark shell of a snapping turtle, wet and glistening, erupts from the water, upturning lily pads, which flash their rose-purple undersides as they cascade off the turtle's back, pulled back into the water by their long, winding stems. The snapper is hunting. The sounds I heard were strikes he made on the other side of the island, attempts to seize frogs, fish—I am not sure what. As I see the shell plow through the lily pads and sedges I picture his great head lowered, just beneath the surface, his massive neck at full reach but ready to recoil and strike with blinding speed. The shell seems a strange, disembodied entity as it turns in a wide arc and crushes deliberately toward the island, emerging even more from the shallows as it does so. More strikes here, several in quick succession, with the sound of a

Floating-leaf pondweed, *Potamogetan natans.*

flattened hand smacking the surface with all its force. I cannot see the turtle's head, but having seen snappers lunge and strike on land and having seen them seize food in captivity, I have a clear vision of what this one is about. Apparently unsuccessful, he backs away from the shoreline, turns, and surges anew with real speed along the edge of the grasses, the crest of his shell shedding water and lily pads. There are several more strikes as he churns his way along, and then, with no pause, the shell begins to submerge and disappears in a swirl of lily pads. He has captured his quarry and is settling to the bottom to eat. The surface closes over and grows still.

A white waterlily bobs back above water and floats serenely on the slender mooring of its stem.

Most turtles, the snapper among them, cannot swallow unless their heads are under water. Exceptions are tortoises and box turtles, which live and feed on land, and several species adapted for feeding on land as well as in the water, such as wood and possibly Blanding's turtles. Spotted turtles have been reported to be able to eat on land, but I have never observed this, and no recent literature supports the claim. Captive specimens will seize food on land and take it to the water for swallowing, even if they put only their heads and necks below the surface. In

all aquatic turtles, the windpipe is located on the floor of the mouth behind an immovable tongue; it can be closed off by a valve to allow swallowing underwater without letting air into the lungs.

Although turtles sometimes rush suddenly at floating or immersed masses of plants in attempts to startle prey into revealing itself, the snapping turtle's aggressive hunting activity was unusual. Perhaps he was pressured by the heat, which raised his metabolism. And food is often less abundant in midsummer than in bountiful spring. With increased energy needs and a dwindling food supply, he may not have been getting enough to eat in his usual style of foraging on the bottom or lying in wait with infinite patience to ambush prey.

It is more common for a snapping turtle to lie motionless in weed-choked shallows, where even a tremendous one is surprisingly undetectable. A certain movement nearby will trigger a strike of awesome speed and accuracy and formidable strength. The snapper's strongly hooked upper and lower jaws take a hold that even large, vigorous prey cannot escape. If the intended prey eludes the strike, the turtle will draw back his neck and settle into his hiding place once again. Ambush may give way to a stealthy approach toward prey. Snapping turtles have a measure and grace in their movements, and when stalking something like a fish they seem to move without moving. Eyes unblinking, the great head turns slowly, imperceptibly, toward its target. I have seen this process be so gradual that I never did detect actual movement; I only observed eventually that the head was in a different position. As the head moves, one forefoot is drawn up and extended in a strategic direction; and the hindfoot on the opposite side shifts and sets with an equally slow and rhythmic motion. The toes and claws, with their pronounced webs, draw together as the imperceptible forward motion is made. The skin and scales along the outer edge of the legs compress; these are spread and flared out as the back stroke is taken. This stalking mode is a super-slow-motion replica of the explosive lunge and strike of the snapping turtle who feels he is close enough to take a shot at his intended dinner. Buoyant in the water, a heavy snapping turtle can move on tiptoes with the nimbleness of a prancing, prowling fox. His long, serpentine neck extends and retracts fluidly; his head is cocked one way, then the other, as the turtle searches for food.

The diet of the snapping turtle and his feeding habits are matters of controversy and some conjecture. It seems surprising for a creature of such rapacious hunting potential to be largely herbivorous, but it has been well documented that in many habitats and situations, half or more of the snapper's diet is composed of plants. It is also evident that these turtles eat dead or injured fish. With their great bulk to feed, they are actually omnivorous, eating anything they can find. The image of these turtles ravaging unchecked through lakes, ponds, and swamps, swallowing up game fish and ducklings, does not bear up under scientific inquiry. Nor is such an image borne out by this species' natural history or the reality of the ecological checks and balances that prevail in the wild. If a snapping turtle's strike is compared to lightning, a healthy fish can be said to be quicksilver in the water. Fish species taken by snapping turtles include carp, suckers, hornpout, perch, and sunfish; the larger and swifter game fish favored by anglers are not eaten in any significant quantity. Snapping turtles can be a benefit to wetland habitats by thinning out overpopulated and stunted fish. Ducks, or any other potential prey, spread out over lakes and marshes with their own well-tested survival techniques, are not in danger of being exterminated by snapping turtles, though one would not care to have such a turtle in a confined duck pond on a farm, any more than one would want a fox in a henhouse or a deer in the garden.

The diets of different turtle species vary as do their habitats.

Eastern box turtle, *Terrapene c. carolina*, **eating an earthworm.**

Blanding's turtle, *Emydoidea blandingii,* **eating a crayfish.**

Most turtles are omnivorous and take varied plant and animal food; and most are opportunistic, consuming what is available when it is available. I once observed a yearling snapper that had just caught a dragonfly larva in a shallow pool. The ferocious-looking larva was larger than the turtle's head and neck combined, and I marvelled that the snapper was able to swallow it completely in the end. One would not think that such a meal could fit within the little turtle's shell. Immediately after his laborious swallowing, the turtle burrowed into the mud beneath him. He was in for a long digestion process. Even in the warm season, turtles can go a long time without eating. They are able to take in a large quantity when fortune provides it and ride out long, hard times.

————————————————

June growth closes over more and more of the silvery surface of the marsh. The heat of the season moves into the water as well as the earth and shimmers in the air. As the mists of dawn disperse, the spotted turtle crawls up to bask in the rushes. Following her nesting, with summer heat building up, she suns herself early in the mornings, in the first hot light to burn through the haze. She no longer surrenders herself to the heat in the trancelike torpor of April noons but is ever alert now, her eyes open to every movement. The endless circlings of dragonflies do not distract her, nor does she take alarm at a swallow skimming her grassy island. But when a great blue heron shifts its stance slightly, she is in the water in an instant, diving swiftly and strongly through the submarine vegetation and digging into the bottom. The heron had been standing as still as the landscape itself when the turtle emerged and climbed onto the edge of the clump of rushes. This watchful hunter had eyes out for fish and frogs. Had the turtle been closer, it might have been worth the great bird's effort to try to seize her and work a breakfast out of her shell.

There is a patience in the marsh. It seems frogs are motionless for days between their lunges at insects. A heron stands like a carved bird for interminable spans of time, only to stalk slowly forward a few steps and take up another long, motionless vigil. A snapping turtle lies unmoving in ambush, as though he had a hundred years to spare. The spotted turtle remains immobile for nearly an hour after scrambling from her sunning place into the dark mud. Then she raises herself into the water and examines the surface above. Nothing moves. Slowly she makes her way upward through tangles of sedge and bur-reed and the winding stems of watershield. Just beneath the surface she stops, and her eyes scan the light of the air above the water. Slowly, without disturbing the placid surface, she extends the tips of her nostrils above the water and breathes. Eventually, she raises her head into the morning air, blinks water away from her eyes, and looks over the great plane of water at her eye level.

She spends the rest of the morning foraging in the shallow water, grazing on strands of algae, taking small snails from the stems of plants, digging down into the deep layers of fallen growth to look for larvae. At times she moves along the surface, or slightly below it, snapping up insects that have fallen there. Her time of mating and nesting has passed. With an

Blue-flag iris, *Iris versicolor*.

aura of timelessness, the long summer extends before her. The season of turning leaves will come, the essential sun will seem to slip away from the earth, and the turtle will have to suspend her life and surrender her world to winter. But that is a distant time, unremembered and unforeseen.

A creature of the sun, she still must avoid its extremes. As the intense heat of July becomes established, she feeds in the first light of morning and in the evening shadows. One morning she moves along a familiar route, over moss and sand, through sweetfern and into alder thickets, crosses a hard-packed dirt road very quickly, and rustles into the tall reedgrass of the swale. The water is shallow, barely covering her shell. At times a scattering of her brilliant spots shows above the surface as she works around the stands of sedge and grass, hunting. Thousands of roots, great and small, and the dry winds and hot sun have taken away the water. Molecule by molecule, the legacy of the winter's snow and the chill April downpours has been carried away. There have not been enough summer rains to replenish the three-acre swale and slow the daily drop in water level. The spotted turtle moves into a deeper-bottomed area, where a foot of water covers her. She threads her way through the tangles of grass and fallen branches from the overhanging alders, willows, and winterberry holly. Here she feeds on mosquito larvae and finds moths and other insects from the land and air that erred in their flights or leaps and became trapped on the water's surface.

As the sun climbs toward its zenith, and heat and light bear directly into the clear shallows of the swale, the spotted turtle moves into a pool beneath a canopy of winterberry holly. The slender trunks of this emergent shrub reach seven feet into the air, lacing it with a layer of leaves. Several great mounds of royal fern spread delicate foliage in the shady retreat beneath the holly, and near the lighter edge of the canopy sprays of swordlike blue-flag iris leaves lance out of the water. High above the water these plants hold a few last flowers, flowers like fragments of the early morning sky fallen to earth and lingering in the shade. Here the turtle hides, close against the sheltering ferns, and waits out the heat of the day.

Great blue heron, *Ardea herodias*.

The sun completes its high, slow arc of the summer day, and long shadows creep across the swale. The spotted turtle slides through the open shallows to the outer edge of the canopy. There is nothing to disturb her in the tapestry of stems and leaves before her, so she moves on out among the stands of reedgrass, for the most part avoiding what little open water there is and keeping under the dense, grassy cover as she searches for food again. The singing of crickets grows louder, and single notes of green frogs erupt as twilight deepens. Song sparrows trail out their final calls of the day here and there across the swale. A tiny star appears in the darkening sky. The water lies still and warm. The turtle digs deep into the center of a grass clump and lodges herself in its embracing roots. The moon comes out, and the hunters of the night move among the shadows of the marsh.

Days of high summer continue to pass, and no rain comes. Water is left standing only in the deepest channel of the swale, which is not more than one hundred feet long and four feet wide. Even here the water is only a few to eight inches deep. Sparrows feed on ripening reedgrass seeds and hunt proliferating grasshoppers. There are few green frogs remaining. As the water shrinks away and the swale undergoes the transition from wetland to dry pasture, frogs move outward in the night. Male spotted turtles who remained in the swale after mating and females who returned to it after nesting have also begun a migration. Taking their signals to disperse and guided by an inner knowledge, a great variety of creatures begin moving out, one by one, along pathways only they can know.

As the first rays of sunlight slant over the high ridge to the east, driving the hunters of the night back into the deeper shadows of the forest, the spotted turtle crawls out of the dwindling water of the swale and sets off on another overland migration. She ascends a knoll topped by young oaks and pines, moves through an open area of bluestem and sweet-fern still wet with dew, then de-scends a slope of shading white pine. She crosses an old logging road, where grasses and wildflowers have moved in to form a long, narrow pasture. A familiar tree line of alders and red maples rises up before her. She finds the beaver channel that is a tunnel through the thicket and slides down its steep slope into the water. Beyond the tree line extends an open sedge meadow that is flooded by the bordering river in the spring and holds water into the dry season due to a beaver dam sev-eral hundred yards downstream. The channel holds several inches of water in the driest of times. Soft mud lies beneath the water-way to a depth of half a foot.

Muskrat passageways and occa-sional pools wind among the sedges, and a deep channel lies along the landward edge, where buttonbush and sweetgale grow.

Here the turtle alternately hunts and hides. There is enough heat in her world now, by day and by night, that she seldom basks. As the days pass, with glaring sun and no rain, the water level steadily drops even in this small marsh. At twilight, as the heat of the day diminishes, the spotted turtle hunts in the sedge shallows at the edge of a pool that connects with the beaver channel. A move-ment in the water catches her eye, and she lowers her head beneath the surface. Among the sunken strands of sedge a dragonfly larva wriggles in search of its own food. With her head extended, she stalks slowly within range of her prey, her shell just breaking the surface. The movement of the tur-tle shell in the twilight water is caught by another pair of eyes. A large raccoon has waded into the warm shallows from the surround-ing woods, stealthily crossing the sedge meadow. He waits until the turtle lowers her head into the water, then slowly stalks in her direction. Preoccupied with her

own quest, she does not detect the advance of the black-masked hunter. He sets his nimble feet in the marshy ground, measures the distance, and makes his rush. A blur of movement catches the cor-ner of the turtle's eye. Her prey is instantly forgotten as she thrusts back hard with all four feet and launches herself into the pool. Clawed feet that would pin her to the slippery mud rake her shell. The raccoon fails to get a grip on the smooth, wet dome of the tur-tle's shell. He surges forward again, up to his armpits in water, furiously groping in the muck. The turtle is gone.

The raccoon flails water and muck for only a moment. He knows there is no finding the tur-tle now. He turns and goes off among the sedges. The turtle re-mains motionless for over an hour, then slips out of the mud and along the bottom to dig up under dense sedge stalks on the far side of the pool. She works her way in-to the tangle to a point at which she can just reach the air under the arching sedges with the tips of her nostrils. She spends the night with-out moving, except for an occa-sional extension of her head to take a breath. White scratches

raked into the back of her carapace mark her narrow escape.

Bladderwort that lifted yellow flowers on threadlike stalks above the water now lies upon mud. Stranded lily pads curl in the afternoon sun. Crickets sing in the sedge, and frogs withdraw to puddles in the densest shade of overhanging buttonbush. Painted turtles, Blanding's turtles, and young snapping turtles who hunted in the spring floods here departed long ago to swim the deeper waters along the river margins or make their own overland migrations to the great marsh. As her world constricts

around her once more, and critical food and water shrink away, the spotted turtle works her way through the cool shallows under the overhanging canopy that reaches out from the bank. She searches among the underwater roots and grass mats, then begins digging in a dark hollow in the tangle of a red maple's anchoring roots. Her shell disappears beneath the mud. She tunnels her way among the roots and works herself into a crevice up under the steep bank of the marsh. She will not be discovered here. As the burning sun wheels overhead and grass edges curl in dry summer

fields, she finds a refuge that seems to hold a measure of the past cold season's chill. She draws herself tightly within her shell, her breathing slows; she enters a sleep almost as deep as that of winter.

Weeks later cloud towers rise high above the mountain and advance steadily from the west. Hazy skies darken in the late afternoon. Rolls of thunder break closer to the marsh with each brilliant flash of lightning. First with a scattering of raindrops and then a deluge, a storm sweeps over the fields and water. Wet leaves reflect a thousand flickering lights with every flash of lightning . . . one great bolt strikes directly over the nesting fields and for a searing white instant burns the color out of the landscape. Rain rushes off the hills, blows in a great sheet across the sandy plains . . . a month of heat and drought is violently overturned by torrents from the sky.

The storm rages for nearly an hour and then rolls away with gradually quieting thunder, leaving a still, leaden sky behind. Rain falls steadily through the night and into the next day. Another round of thunderstorms erupts in the restless air, and

Sphagnum moss, *Sphagnum sp.*

more rain beats down. Every root
rejoices, every leaf uncurls and
flushes full once more, with water
surging within and soaking steadily from without. Cracked mud
softens and heals as water collects
above it. Trickles and then rivulets
trace out a hundred tiny waterways forgotten since spring.

Just as it had seemed it would
never rain again, it seems the rain
will never stop. Days pass, with
drizzle and downpour shattered by
thunderstorms in the night. And
then a quieting sky, with a trailing
edge of cloud slipping away in the
east, unveils the sun of a late
afternoon. A song sparrow sings.

The river cannot carry away the
runoff from the rains quickly
enough; it floods and spills its
banks, washing into surrounding
swales and marshland. Above the
beaver dam, even more water is held
back and spreads into surrounding
hollows and wetlands. Lily pads
that lay on coiled stems on top of
mud are now tethered under two
inches of water.

Water rises up against the steep
bank of the marsh and floods into
the earth under the bank. Much
as the spring thaw helped to awaken
the spotted turtle to a new season,
the flooding of the midsummer

rainy spell signals her that a new
season within a season has come.
She winds her way from beneath
the flooded bank and swims to the
surface. She clings to the shore.
The water here is too deep for her
now. Painted turtles will soon be
cruising among the pondweed that
will have to unwind and extend
slender stems to lay floating leaves
back up on the surface.

Even as the rains were falling,
frogs were moving in the night.
They were the first of a living tide

to return to the swale. From hidden shallows along the river margin
or dark hollows where they have
been estivating, other spotted
turtles will soon be on the move.
In a day or so, young painted and
snapping turtles, and perhaps a
Blanding's turtle, will appear in
the flooded reedgrass as though
they had come from nowhere. The
spotted turtle crawls up the bank,
crosses a grassy logging trail, and
begins her ascent of the knoll on
her way back to the swale.

Chapter Five

HATCHING

The shivering mountains turn to indigo;
The autumn stream flows murmuring all day long.
—Wang Wei

25 August, 12 noon. *After several chill nights and cool autumnal days, the sun is full and hot as I stand in the waters of the cove of the Great Marsh. In the low 50's this morning, with periods of cloud cover and strong winds. The day warms up at last. Bur-reed and sedge dance on the strong sweeps of the departing Canadian air — it will be difficult to detect any turtle movements. Cricket song is very loud and prevails over even the strongest surges of wind in the pines on the eastern shore. A large painted turtle is basking on a stump in the middle of the cove, a young one rests at the surface on a thick mat of waterweeds.*

White waterlily and yellow pond lily are still in bloom, and the last stalks of pickerelweed are still adorned with purple flowers, though the plants look weary, late in their season. Bumblebees take heavy flights across the water to reach the pickerelweed and the water smartweed, which lifts conspicuous rosered and bright pink flower stalks out of the water among goldtipped sedges. The plants of this cove take on autumnal tones. One never sees summer slip from the marsh; the turning seems at once sudden and gradual . . . a bronzing comes to the greens of grass and sedge, woolgrass turns a deeper brown and its seeding head goes densely woolly. The marsh St. Johnswort bloomed yesterday, it seems, yet today carries deepred seed capsules, its leaves rosepurple. Heavy pods split open on the arching stalks of blue-flag, revealing columns of red-brown seeds. Thick discs are stacked like coins in a change sorter . . . they are an ancient coinage of a future growth, to be dispensed one at a time among the sedgy shallows of the wetland. I look back to the gleam of sunlight on the painted turtle's shell and try to think of summer only.

Gold has touched the three-way sedge, and maroons, oranges, and reds creep into the floating leaves of the watershield I wade through as I make a search of the shallows. I don't know where he came from, but suddenly a hatchling painted turtle is swimming rapidly through the water; I see him in a clear space in the watershield and lunge for him before he disappears beneath its covering leaves. It is certainly a newborn turtle I pull out of the mossy, submerged growth; his carapace is just over an inch long and equally wide at its widest point. A sharp, tiny white eggtooth sticks out from his upper jaw, just beneath his nose. I turn him over and admire the deep golden yellow of his plastron and the brilliant red on the under margins of his carapace. This is the earliest date on which I have ever found a hatchling turtle and makes me think I ought to start my search for them even earlier next year. This tiny one may have been sunning himself on the floating watershield and taken flight into the water at my heronlike approach. Even just out of the

Yellow waterlily, *Nuphar variegatum.*

egg, turtles take to the sun and must reconcile this need with the one to keep hidden.

31 August. *I am sad to number the final day of this month. After the deluge of yesterday, clearing skies, intense blue, with wisps and swirls of cirrus clouds . . .*

Seed pod, blue-flag iris.

low 70's. Clear, light breezes dancing from every quarter, it seems. Glimmering aspen leaves, swaying pines. . . .

I have made my rounds of these fields every day since coming upon the hatchling painted turtle out in the cove but have found no baby turtles nor any sign of hatching. I examine the ground even more minutely now than I did in the nesting season . . . what I look for is even harder to find. My search takes me past the many nests dug up in spring. They are not such scars now; summer rains have washed sand and dirt back into the excavations and softened their edges, so that they have become shallow depressions, and the eggshells that remain scattered around them have been dried up by the sun and pulverized by wind and rain, so they are not so glaringly evident. In time, they will become one with the sand they lie upon. Although it is upsetting at the time, there is a certain mercy in the destruction of life at so early a moment for most turtles. Baby birds do not often have it so easy, nor do tadpoles or salamander larvae. Turtles who

make it to hatching certainly face hazards, but late-season predation is not as widespread as the rampant carnage that accompanies nesting season. That great depletion reduces possible nest finds at hatching time to an effort of such diminishing returns that predators are not so attracted to take up the search—although the diggings I find here and there attest to the fact that they never abandon it. The few surviving nests are scattered, and the hatchings occur at widely separated, unpredictable times—one nest could emerge in August and another in April or May of the following year. Even when a nest does hatch, it might launch one turtle today, another a week or more later. If I had been depending on baby turtles to be my food this week of walking the fields, I would have lost considerable weight. The odds take a turn in the turtles' favor.

Turtles always do manage to slip a nest or two past the predators of their eggs. Having watched a skunk prowl, eyes, nose, and tongue close to the ground, and even in the ground, in its ceaseless crisscrossing, rooting, retracing steps, searching anew every square inch in a large area of field, and

knowing that he returns at dusk night after night and prowls until dawn, I can only marvel that any mother turtle is able to leave a nest that will succeed in reproducing her kind. One wonders if luck or skill is at work, if it is no more than a numbers game. All factors are surely involved, but with one hundred eighty million nesting seasons behind them, turtles must be accorded credit for something other than luck.

At two o'clock in the afternoon I come upon a scene I have spent many weeks over six turtle seasons looking for: a hatchling spotted turtle rests on a tuft of spare moss growing on sand. Appropriately enough, he is close by a tuft of bluestem. For the first time, I have a record of a time and a place, here in this extensive paludal realm of the spotted turtle, for a newly hatched spotted turtle's journey to the water. The joy of finding him at such a telling point in his life history is reward enough for my hours of walking and searching. I get close to the warm earth and look at him. His carapace is black and, typical of these hatchlings, has one yellow spot on each shield. In time, many more spots will appear. He hasn't a speck of dirt or a grain of sand on him. Perhaps he has lost any trace of these in travelling, or maybe he was washed clean by yesterday's heavy rain, as he hid beneath a clump of bluestem to wait out the night, his journey not yet completed. His caruncle is still there, the eggtooth that may have helped him break out of his egg; and he still carries a mark on his plastron where recently there was a remnant of yolk-sac.

I try to ascertain which direction he has come from, and search the ground minutely, but find neither nest nor sibling. I mark the spot where I found him. Possibly his mother dug her nest quite near the two I observed, escaping my notice and the intense scrutiny of the skunks. From the hatchling's location and apparent direction, I would assume the marsh to be his destination, so I carry him there and set him in the shallows.

Upon completing their nests on that same morning last June, the two spotted turtles I was watching headed toward the dense thickets of the Great Swale, walking directly away from the Great Marsh. Would their hatchlings head back into the Great Swale, a difficult, drier, and more distant environment in the fall, or head into the cove of the Great Marsh, which would seem to be a perfect nursery for hatchling turtles of any aquatic species? Before now, the only hatchling spotted turtle I ever found in the Digs was one I caught in mid-April, in the cove. But in years of wading there, I have never found a juvenile. There is a further perplexity in that the only juvenile I have found in the Digs was one I caught early on an evening in spring in one of the small, winding channels of the Great Swale. As well known as young spotted turtles are for keeping hidden, I am at a loss as to why I have found only two in the Digs. I had better luck in tracking hatchlings and juveniles in the cranberry bogs and shallow wetlands of south coastal New England.

From what little I have seen in the Digs, it seems possible that some surviving hatchlings head for environments such as the cove of the Great Marsh and over time make migrations to the other wetland habitats that abound here. I have seen spotted turtles come from both the Great Swale and the Great Marsh to nest within a few yards of where I have found this little traveller; it would be interesting to know if the hatchlings from these nests headed off in directions their respective mothers had come from more than three months before, or if they all simply headed for the nearest, most obvious source of water. Where turtles emerging from nests far away from these fields and its nearby marsh may head, or where any of the young ones may live during those precarious seven to ten years until they reach adulthood, is a mystery I may never fully solve, but one I hope to gain insights into during future years of wading these wetlands and watching their turtles.

7 September, late afternoon. *I sit on one of the oak stumps in the Digs, almost in the middle of the dirt road that bisects the nesting fields, and scan the open earth, looking for any movement, any sign of a hatchling making its journey from nest to water. The sky, so open here, is a clear September blue. A steady but warm and benign wind blows. It keeps two constant songs, one in the flickering leaves of aspens that border the field, another in the pines among the aspens and on the surrounding hills. Cricket song never ceases. The bluestem is bleached and bronzy, brushed with soft rose-purples. The diminutive gray goldenrod stands here and there throughout the open fields, its deep-yellow flower heads crooked like tiny shepherd staffs. The only creature I have seen this afternoon is a good-sized blacksnake that had come out to hunt on the sparse surface of the field beyond the aspens. When he saw me, he slid quickly, heavily and noisily, back into the brush beneath the trees.*

It is glorious here. Time seems held in place. I am mesmerized . . . words like *trance* and *dazed* come to mind. The swamps have done this to me as far back as I can remember. I cannot describe the feeling that seems to swim in my head, the way my eyes drift and see without being able to focus.

There is pleasure in the afternoon's slow passage. By imperceptible degrees, the hours turn into evening. By imperceptible degrees, the year turns toward winter. The long, cool shadows, and the small blue asters aglow in them, are signs in the season's calendar. The days of the turtle season are no longer without number. A finiteness touches them as autumn tinges touch the hills and slip across the marsh. It becomes harder to leave now. I have not yet turned to go, and already I want to come back.

Bluestem grass, *Andropogon scoparius.*

9 September. *To the Digs at 2:30 PM. A cold spell has passed, but it brought the first touches of frost and has left its mark. It is no longer a summer landscape that surrounds the marsh, although uncommonly hot September weather has moved in — it is 90 degrees. Autumn light and summer heat lie beneath thin brush strokes of cloud in the sky. The wind is hot and uneasy. It swirls among the pines and sweeps across the sand, stirring the grass and goldenrod as if it knows it cannot stay.*

Slowly I search the fields, as I have so many times on many afternoons of hatching seasons. I read the earth again, as I do at the time of the turtles' nesting. Certain small stones become very familiar to me. I know where a dragonfly's wing rests in the grass. There are no new signs in the earth or moss. I close out my day's search with a final walk around the rim of the deep sand-pit, circling it in the opposite direction from my approach of an hour before. I am surprised to find an exit hole I had missed. Sometimes it takes a different angle, a different slant of the sun, to reveal a secret of the marsh. This is the opening of a snapping turtle's nest, the discrete form that holds its narrow, oval shape even in pure sand after the hatchling turtles have opened and departed through it upon leaving their nest. I dig down into the nest and find nine turtles at the bottom of the egg chamber. One egg has failed to develop, and one hatchling, who made it out of his eggshell, has died in the nest. From the eggshells in the chamber I calculate that at least twenty little snapping turtles have already left the nest. Each hatchling is a miniature replica of the great turtle who stalked across this sand in June, anchored herself on the steep south-facing slope, and dug into the sand. The tails of the hatchlings are disproportionately long, but with their tiny spikes they reflect the powerful appendage with which their mother reached down into the earth and deposited the eggs that cradled them all summer long. On their undersides, the baby turtles are black, flecked with white streaks and spots, a coloration that will fade in two or three years. Their plastrons bear fresh scars at the site of their yolk-sacs, and each

Gray goldenrod, *Solidago nemeralis*.

turtle carries an eggtooth on the point of his upper jaw.

After placing the nine turtles in a large paper bag and anchoring it against the steady drift of wind, I go down into the sandpit to see if any of those who left the nest might still be around. There is no sign of them here or on the surrounding plane . . . they may have tunneled out yesterday or earlier this afternoon; in any event, they have made it to the water by now and are hidden in the marsh.

I return to the nest site on the ridge to retrieve the living treasures I dug out of the earth. As I take up the bag and my walking stick, I catch sight of a hatchling snapping turtle tumbling down the slope about seven feet away . . . I just barely notice the movement out of the corner of my eye. Wondering how I could possibly have missed this one in the nest, or how he could have emerged and stayed so close by, I go to get the turtle. My wonderings are answered within an instant. At my feet, the earth moves. The head of a hatchling snapper emerges from the sandy crust. The turtle blinks away some sand and takes his first long look at the world. Another head appears be-

hind the first. As a third head appears, I drop to my knees. Over years of walking nesting fields I have looked for such a moment: to be present at the hatching of a turtle nest out in the wild. A fourth head thrusts up through the sand. The turtles look around for several moments, then begin shouldering their way through the earth's dry crust.

One hatchling moves out onto the sand. His head has dried, as has his carapace at the shoulder margin. He is dusted with a pale powder of fine sand and looks at once newborn and aged. Already an ancient wisdom is at work in his hours-old head as he cranes his long, dusty neck and contemplates what he is able to see of the universe. The one-and-one-eighth-inch turtle rubs sand grains from his eyelids with a foreleg and blinks his dark, wet eyes clear in the afternoon light. His half-open, liquid eyes are emphasized dramatically by the dusty earth caked around them. A picture returns to my mind, of a June dawn six years ago, when I first saw a snapping turtle nesting on this same expanse. The first rays of sunlight were touching the far end of the field, mists swirled over the pale

earth and around the great turtle, obscuring all but the tops of surrounding pines. As the sun crept over the land and touched her dark shell, the turtle rose high on her legs and, dragging her spiked tail across the freshly dug ridge of sand atop her nest, stalked off toward the marsh, still shrouded in shadow and fog. She could have been a dinosaur moving through the total silence of that morning hour. That moment, and the moment of the hatchling now before me, struck me as many of my turtle encounters have, as though they were scenes from the dawn of time.

The hatchling's pause for reflection is brief. He has a direction, and heads off, standing high on four little legs, dragging a spiked, one-inch tail behind him. The others follow, strongly, quickly; sometimes three or four at a time, with as many as seven at a time having heads and shoulders, or just heads, at the opening of their nest. As the turtles shoulder upward and outward, I see how the characteristic exit hole is formed. Their arching, thrusting necks, straining legs, and pressing shells open the earth and pack it into a firm, oval doorway as they struggle out. After the first ten or so emerge, the door is open for the following siblings. Upon climbing out of the dark hole in the earth, each turtle pauses and seems to ponder. Each has his own chelonian reckoning to do in his initial minutes of life above ground, deciphering the brilliant light and dazzling landscape before him.

After his moment of stillness in the light, each turtle heads toward the water he cannot see. If I were to stand up, even I would not be able to see any trace of the Great Marsh from this vantage point, and I am a skyscraper compared to these turtles. Yet they seem to know the way, and there they head, though some take a roundabout route at first. The third hatchling out of the nest turns directly away from the steep incline of the great ditch, which means directly away from the distant, unseen marsh. I watch with interest, to see if this little one might have some other destination in mind. But after travelling several feet across the bare earth in a straight line, with his back to the water, the tiny turtle begins to make a slow arc around the rim of the open sandpit, toward the beckoning shallows. As the turtles emerge from their nest, several take this route, though the majority plunge directly down the steep, seven-foot embankment. They will have to ascend an equally high, steep slope on the other side of the sandpit. These turtles apparently are of the

Exit hole, snapping-turtle nest.

straight-line, shortest-distance, shortest-time school, and, disregarding the precipitous nature of the terrain, make a beeline for the nearest water.

I wish that I could magically follow each in his path to the safety of the pond, as they begin to spread out over the course of their seventy-five-yard journey. I wish even for invisibility, that I might learn the fate of each of these turtles, whatever that fate may be, under completely natural conditions, as he makes his potentially treacherous way across the open expanse of the field. This being impossible, I scoop up the little turtles when they have scrambled several feet from the exit hole, to take home and observe for a time. The following ranks are oblivious to my picking up the forerunners; it's no good for them to return to the nest or try to hide in their shells, no matter how voracious a predator I might be. There is no cover for them now; they can only head for the water. I take the last turtles from the nest and have a total of thirty. Every egg in this nest has produced a perfect, viable hatchling. It will be a joy to return in a day or two and release these turtles to their destiny in the marsh.

The turtle's nest and egg chamber form a shelter in the earth for developing embryos. They are shielded by a covering of sand or soil ranging in depth from about an inch to six or seven inches, depending on the size and species of the mother. The surrounding earth protects turtles from extremes of temperature and keeps them from becoming too wet or dry during their incubation. Turtle embryos possess wide tolerances but do seem to require periods of high environmental temperatures (in excess of 72° F.) during incubation in order to develop properly. The eggshell itself, with its tough membranes and chalky mineral layer, protects the embryo from desiccation, although prolonged heat and drought can lead to a fatal drying out. It also stands as a barrier against biotic elements; turtle eggs are remarkably resistant to contamination by bacteria and fungi.

Eggs that escape predation and are spared or survive environmental extremes carry embryos through to the time of pipping, the turtle's breaking of his eggshell, which in most species occurs one to four days before the hatchling digs his way out of the nest. At the time of pipping, gelatinous sheaths that have covered the sharp edges of the embryo's shell margin, claws, and eggtooth, fall away. The eggtooth is not a true tooth but a horny thickening on the point of the upper jaw, which can help the turtle break open the front end of his eggshell. It is lost within a week following hatching. Once the hatchling tears the eggshell open, he begins to uncurl and spread out from the fetal position, assuming his normal shape. His plastron, which has been curled around the yolk, unfolds and flattens, and this action helps draw the yolk-sac into the hatchling's shell at the umbilicus. As the remaining yolk is withdrawn, it contributes to the filling out of the baby turtle, who is quite egg-shaped at the moment of pipping. At this point, with most species, the hatchling is not quite ready to crawl out of the remnant eggshell, let alone dig out of the nest.

Not all of the hatchlings of a nest necessarily emerge at once. One wind-blown day in mid-September last season, when it was so cold I wore a heavy coat over my swamp vest as I checked the turtle nests, I found a solitary painted-turtle hatchling struggling under one of the screens. He was facing the marsh that was some fifty yards distant, out of his sight. I lifted the covering and freed the little one. No opening in the earth was left to show his point of departure from the nest. I was certain that several siblings were lying there, beneath that shallow covering of earth, perfectly hatched and ready to move, but waiting. Their impulse to leave the nest would not come until the other side of winter. But this one had been prompted to dig out on such an unlikely day for any turtle movement, though close to the ground it was considerably warmer than the wind in which I stood. He would be taking his chances on surviving his first winter somewhere in the shallows of the marsh; the others would hold to the nest through the long freezing of the earth and the eventual thaw. After fixing the screen securely back in place, I carried the eager hatchling to the cove and set him down in the sphagnum shallows among the wind-riffled sedges.

I have no way of knowing his fate, but I do know that of his fellows who remained in the nest; all died over the winter. I waited until the thirteenth of May the following spring and dug into the nest. Five hatchlings were there, perfectly formed, so lifelike it seemed at any moment they would open their eyes, blink those blinks of just-hatched turtles, and scramble forth in search of the marsh. They were so fresh, their limbs flexible and their eyes not the least bit sunken, no scent of death about them, that I took them home thinking that they might still be in a dormant state and yet spring to life. But they had perished; their commitment to the nest had proved fatal over that particular winter. It may have been that an unusual, snowless winter in this northern wetland, combined with a prolonged deep freeze, had taken them beyond their limits. From their condition, I would say they had died during their hibernation, perhaps even close to the end of it. It was interesting to me that they had survived the equally unusual heat and drought of the preceding summer, but I am sure that in mid-September they were as alive as the one who had tunneled out.

As for that one, he, too, would have had a difficult time with the ensuing winter conditions. Perhaps he made it through. The ice penetrated deeply into the substrate of the marsh and held solid there weeks after the water had melted, a situation I had not encountered here before. Had there been a sufficient snow cover over land and water alike, all of these turtles might have lived, and a single painted-turtle nest would have produced autumn and spring emergents.

In cases of synchronous emergence, all the hatchlings leave the nest at close to the same time, sometimes on one another's heels. But asynchronous emergence, in which hatchlings depart on separate days, may be more common. The last turtle may make his move more than a week after his first sibling to leave the nest has been in the water. This aspect of behavior in freshwater turtles appears to be rather unpredictable, and for many species specific data are lacking. With snapping- and eastern-painted-turtle nests I have observed, there seems to be a tendency for hatchlings to clear out all at once, sea-turtle-like, though some may wait behind for a second rush to the water; and I have witnessed a nest of snappers hatch out over a period of three days.

Out of the egg, and finally out of the earth, each hatchling faces

Hatchling painted turtle pipping from egg that has been removed from nest.

the overland journey to the water. This is no great challenge for a species like the musk turtle, which tends to nest right along the shoreline, or for hatchlings of mothers who have buried their eggs within a few feet of the water. (I have found painted-turtle nests on a beaver lodge not far above the water line.) But most turtles wander far and wide to find a nesting site to their liking, and their inch-long hatchlings face a journey of hundreds of yards. Before this travel begins, in his first moments out of the earth, at the same instant his eyes are flooded with light, each turtle must begin to discover the route to the water. Whatever he reads in the message-laden maze of lights, shadow-shapes, and distances revealed to him during his first steps, the turtle needs to discern the direction of the protecting, nurturing water. The time of day of hatching, the weather conditions, and the condition of the hatchling may result in journeys that take more than a day, with periods of time spent in hiding.

A keen sense of vision plays a vital role in the ability of fresh-water turtles to locate water upon hatching. The same senses that guide migrations and homing in older turtles are probably already at work in the hatchlings, before they have ever seen or felt the water that will become the medium for their lives. An ability to distinguish brightness and color no doubt helps them, as does an instinct to move away from dark shapes of tree masses and geographical features such as ridges and hills, even in the dark. It is possible that newly emerged turtles can detect moisture gradients or even smell water. More obscure factors, such as a sensitivity to temperature or magnetic fields, also may be at work. With immeasurably long evolutionary and genetic ties to signals from the sun and earth, air and water, hatchling turtles have many possible cues to guide them on the critical first migration of their potentially long lives.

Another remarkable aspect of turtle hatching is that some do have the capacity for overwintering in the nest. In some cases this is related to the vagaries of prevailing temperatures over a season of incubation; in others it reflects a deliberate way of dealing with the environment or evading the relentless predation to which turtles are subject. The timing of autumn or spring emergence has genetic as well as environmental components; a hatchling may be "programmed" to wait out the winter in the nest, no matter how favorable the summer incubation period or the autumn above the nest. Some northern populations survive a short, cool summer by overwintering as advanced embryos or as hatchlings; yet populations far to the south may remain in their nests until the following spring even though they had time and warmth enough to develop fully and make a fall emergence. For these turtles, the conditions prevailing in the wet spring are far more favorable than those of the hot, drought-plagued autumn. A hatchling in the latter circumstance would not be able to find the shallow, weed-choked waters necessary for his survival and growth. The autumn and winter environment in the nest beneath the earth, while not without its hazards, is safer than that of the world above ground, and the turtles have the resources to stay in place an extra half year or so and dig out at the time of propitious spring rains. From

north to south, varying among species and within populations of the same species, in concert with or independent of the climate of any one season, some turtles leave the nest in the fall, and others await spring, another expression of behavioral plasticity in an animal that might seem on first inspection to be statically primitive, fixed in time and place.

Individually and collectively, turtles are able to take life's limits to remarkable degrees. The capacity for a hatchling to overwinter in the nest, coupled with the ability of the females of some turtle species to retain viable sperm for four years or so could produce an extension of biological limits that would seem unimaginable. A turtle could mate one season, and four springs later, if she had not encountered a male over the intervening breeding seasons, still produce fertile eggs as a result of that mating. These eggs could lie in the nest through the summer and produce hatchlings that overwinter in the nest. Baby turtles could emerge the following spring, scramble to the water, and take up life there, the progeny of a mating that took place five years before.

14 September. *In a light rain on a cooling afternoon, the temperature descending from the low 70's to the mid-60's, I make my rounds of the nests. At 3:55, as I inspect the remaining spotted-turtle nest, I see the edge of a shell and a tiny foreleg thrusting at the earth's surface. This hatchling must have just broken through the crust over his nest; I believe that I have an opportunity to witness a virtually natural hatching of spotted turtles.*

The other spotted-turtle nest that I had covered, dug on the same day in early June, hatched six days ago. When I came upon it in midafternoon, the top hatchling had dug back into the emergence hole under the screen, his dirt-covered carapace showing. Beneath him, three other hatchlings were huddled. There was one undeveloped egg, with little material left in it, only large and small maggots. I took the four hatchlings home, to record their head and neck patterns, then released them in the marsh nearest their nest the following day.

Now I remove the screen, retreat several paces, and lie down on the sand behind a thin veil of bluestem. At one minute past four, the first hatchling lurches out of the earth. A clump of dried moss, part of his mother's camouflaging of three months before, rolls off his tiny carapace and falls back into the hole. After a brief pause, he walks to a blue-stem clump several feet away and tunnels into the swirls of dried grass at its base. His small journey was to the east. The marsh lies to the south, over one hundred fifty yards distant. A second head appears at the exit hole. When I move slightly to shift my vantage point, this turtle draws his head back into the nest like a turtle submerging. In a moment he reappears, however, and travels less than a foot from the nest before disappearing behind a small wild strawberry plant and a tuft of moss. Ten minutes later a third head appears, looking toward the northwest. This turtle retreats into the nest, and for nearly half an hour nothing further develops with any of them. Tiny mosquitoes, brought out by recent autumn rains, plague me through my motionless vigil, though they are not the affliction I suffered when I watched the mother of these little ones com-

plete her nesting. A slight shifting of the earth, the reappearance of a head, and then nothing. A little over an hour has passed since I first came upon this scene. I surrender to the gathering gloom and increasing rain and uncurl from my position on the ground. I do not believe my hidden presence has been a factor in this hatching drama, or lack of drama; these slow events would have unfolded the same way had there been no screen and no observer, I am quite certain. Apparently there is not always the mad scramble for the water that I had expected . . . there are vagaries in all of this.

I thought that turtle number two had tunneled out of sight close by the plants that obscured him from my view, but I find him resting on the open turf, rain-wet and unmoving, only eight inches from the nest. He had been there just minutes short of an hour. Turtle number three is now in plain sight, sitting in the opening atop the nest. This must surely be a hazardous situation for these hatchlings. Any predator finding one of the conspicuous turtles would have little trouble locating the nest and any turtles that lie within. Turtle number two has

something of the appearance of a runt, and he still holds the shape of the eggshell he so recently left, his carapace quite curved along the spine and curled under at the margins. I take turtle number three from the nest and find a fourth beneath him. This one, quite vigorous apparently, is digging back into the earth, having been disturbed by my dislodging of the one above him. I remove him and finger into the nest, where I come upon an egg, still firmly in place in the hard-packed dirt. I work the egg free and find that it holds a live hatchling who has made very little progress compared with his siblings. The eggshell is torn at the fore edge, and two front feet are barely showing; his head is drawn back, well within his own shell. Surely he would not have made it out of the nest today.

There is so much vulnerability implicit in this protracted emergence from the nest I am sure that many hatchlings are lost in this process, which cannot always go like clockwork. Gathering up the four hatchlings, including the one still within his eggshell, I seek out the first adventurer, who has travelled about four feet and is clearly the Odysseus of this clutch. He is not visible in the bluestem tangles. I pull them away and find him buried into the sandy earth a bit, head down, facing the opposite way from which he had entered his temporary shelter. Something in the situation, perhaps the time of day or the weather conditions, advised him to hide at once and await another day for his quest for the water. This tactic could well have enabled him to escape detection by a predator that might have come upon the open nest.

I carry these five hatchlings back to the house, where I place the one who is yet encased in his eggshell in a bowl of shallow water and watermoss. He makes no move. After some minutes I pick him up and peel the eggshell slightly away from the fore edge of his exposed carapace, and suddenly, in liberation or in terror, he leaps forward and is out of the constraining shell, resting in my hand. He is decidedly egg-shaped. He scrambles vigorously, unfolding as he does so, and is quick to scurry out of sight beneath the watermoss. All of these turtles, however languid they may have appeared as I withdrew them

from my zippered vest pocket, dug rapidly out of sight in the mass of aquatic plants the moment they came into contact with it. I will release them soon in the most logical place I can find, and entrust them to their marsh. Diminutive, brightly decorated spotted-turtle hatchlings may look like tiny ornaments that would fare better in a jewel box than in the hunting grounds of the great blue heron, but their heritage indicates a capacity for survival that will not easily be undone.

There are perplexities for one who would interfere, with however benign intentions, in the matters of nature. It is best to leave the natural processes space and freedom from intervention; and for the most part in my turtle searchings I am an observer. Too many parts of the world have become overpopulous, however, and, with little or no wild space left, human beings must sometimes intervene to keep a species going. The least desirable option becomes the only option. I would prefer to cover only a few nests and not to have to transfer any from their original place in the wild. Deep motorcycle ruts in the nesting fields, which I discovered on my check of nests

Hatchling spotted turtles.

there yesterday, reminded me that no place is left entirely alone, that there are those who have no awareness of, if not an utter disregard for, the sandy domain of turtle nests, bluestem and sweetfern, and the silence the deer and the marsh hawk need. We are thought strange to ask for quiet in our own name and stranger yet to ask it on behalf of the marsh.

19 September. *Though shadows lengthen early across the nesting fields, it is warm, near 80 degrees. I left here in the mid-afternoon yesterday, as cool rain moved in, after checking the nests and picking some cranberries at the far end of the Swale. These berries are flecked and tinged with their own deep red, strewn across the dark sphagnum and held up among the shorter sedges. I remembered a spotted turtle I had caught there, after the monsoons of mid-July, when the green berries were suspended in a foot of water. Warm as it has been, it could drop below freezing any night now, and I wanted to gather cranberries before they got touched by frost. Rain came in the night, and heavy mists in the morning.*

This is the twenty-fifth straight day I have come here. In making my rounds of covered nests I come to the depression left by a predator that had dug into the site of what I believed to be a snapper nest, which I have been watching since June. All is the same as it has been in each day's passing, except for a dark, oval hole in the earth. A nest full of snappers has moved out without disturbing a grain of sand. Only an opening two inches by an inch and a sixteenth bears witness. I head toward the edge of the marsh and circle back toward the nest to see if I can intercept any turtles on their march to the water, but they are gone. Digging into the nest chamber and carefully lifting out and counting the empty eggshells, I come to a total of forty. There are no undeveloped eggs, no dead hatchlings; this was a case of one hundred percent and, I am certain, synchronous hatching. So, there was a nest here after all, one that came very close to being unearthed shortly after it was constructed. I see for myself how one nest escaped the efforts of a predator and flourished through a summer in the Northeast that was marked by greater

than customary extremes, to provide the marsh with a new generation of snapping turtles.

Light from the lowering sun glows in the gold, bronze, and purple bluestem. I take a different route out of the nesting fields, along a mossy pathway that winds along the edge of the thickets, leaving my footprints among the footprints of the deer. No further signs of hatching.

20 September. *More snapping turtles for the Digs . . . a nest is hatching out beneath one of my protective screens as I come upon it at five in the afternoon. Seven turtles prowl in the tight space beneath the screen; two have their heads raised through the quarter-inch mesh, anxious, no doubt, to be on their way to the water. Still packed tightly within the nest chamber, although out of their eggshells, are twenty-five turtles, so compacted at such a late hour in the day, that I doubt they would have left the nest this afternoon. The advance seven would have hit the water in little time, the nest being fifty yards or so from the marsh's border. A second exodus might have occurred tomorrow. Once I extract them, the* *nestbound twenty-five are just as anxious to be on their way as the original seven. Fifteen obviously undeveloped, moribund-looking eggs remain in the chamber; they have a yellowish cast and are deeply indented. I take some photographs (there is not time to draw thirty-two turtles) and then wade the shallows, setting the turtles in widely separated points among the late-season sedges.*

21 September. *To the shallows of the cove of the Great Marsh to release hatchlings . . . I have a fine assortment to add to the marsh's own secret hatch: spotted turtles, painted turtles, and snapping turtles. These, and the wood turtles I will carry to their thicketed brook, are the sons and daughters of nests I relocated in June. Berries are bright red on the winterberry holly along the channel below the bridge and in the Swale, which is damp but has no standing water now. The celadon greens and deep blues of the silky dogwood's heavy clusters of berries hang from the edges of thickets and waterways, their deep-red stems bending nearly to the earth in some places. These are the conspicuous fruits of the season. The cranberries and wild apples have to be sought out. Reaching up with my walking stick, I knock two little apples from the tree that threads its way to light among the alders opposite the Swale; one apple I eat, the other I leave for the mice. Last year this tree had a crop of three apples; this abundant year there are nearly a dozen, though they are small.*

I step into the shallows, and, as I turn him loose in the marsh his mother came from, a snapping-turtle hatchling seems to recognize something in the ankle-deep water he has never seen before. I set the snappers and spotted turtles in the shallowest water, several yards from one another, then wade out a little deeper to release the painted turtles. The tips of the water-smartweed leaves are a vibrant clear yellow.

Hatchling turtles I have released over the years have shown two prevailing modes upon being set into their native home for the first time. Some kick down into the vegetation the instant their plastrons touch the marsh, and disappear. Other turtles become immobile on the surface. As if in a trance, they look out over the water, though their vista may be a matter of inches, their horizon a maze of sedge a few shell lengths away. They seem to have a need to absorb the world around them before they can make a move.

As I take them, one at a time, from the container in which I have carried them to the Digs, each one appears to see something, scent or sense something, as he sits in my hand before I lower him to the water. It is always moving to see how they read the light—the light in the air, on and among the water plants, reflected from the surface of the water. When they see the surface, they seem to know the light beneath it. They become extremely alert—I can see a reaction in them. Is something being imprinted? For years I have wondered what they interpret from their surroundings and have wished for one moment to have their perception of the wonderful natural world that is their home.

I hold each turtle in my open hand a moment. I will never see most of these turtles, perhaps not one of them, again. There are two that I will be able to recognize if they grow and I encounter them

Hatchling snapping turtles under screen.

in a future season—two spotted turtles whose irregular arrangements of carapace plates are recorded in one of my notebooks. These structural patterns will stay with them through their lives. Their shells in time will gain a scattering of many yellow spots, but for now I record the patterns on their heads and necks, which I do not think will change. I do not mark the turtles I release, though it would be interesting to see when and where I might come upon survivors in future years. Wading from several feet to several yards between release points, I continue to place new turtles in the marsh. And what do I look for, intervening human who would be beneficent Pan, as I make my own search in the light, the water, and the plants, seeking the "right" place to set down a hatchling turtle to begin its life in the wild?

I set a painted turtle in the water, on mossy growth that lies just below the surface. He stretches out his neck, shifts his head as though tracking a scent. In a matter of seconds the little turtle shoots his head forth and snaps vigorously onto a trailing piece of water moss. He makes no eating gestures, but just holds on tightly with his jaws. He releases this vegetation after a minute or two, moves forward slightly, and ferociously latches on to the submerged section of a rush's stem. He can hardly get his jaws around the stem but holds fast awhile. At length he lets go his hold, slides off a bit through the water, and launches into white roots of mermaid weed with his tiny jaws. In this way he takes his first hold on his world, and I can only wonder what taste this nascent turtle has for his environment.

Those turtles who dive immediately into water plants but resurface before I move on, and those who stay at the surface when I place them in the water, are oblivious to my presence. In the wild marsh, there is safety in complete stillness. If I reach down and touch one of the motionless meditators, he springs into action at once, dives and disappears. I am certain that after a short time here, probably within their first hours, these turtles would make such a dive at every sudden movement.

I wade on through the shallows, among plants well known to me, plants that will in a day or two become even more familiar to the hatchlings. For a time, the surface of the marsh holds a summer light. The afternoon drones in my ear like an insect. Eight hatchling spotted turtles, living jewels that I have set in a vast land-and-water scape, will be among the turtles sleeping their first night in the star-reflecting water of the marsh. The sun will be their morning star.

———————— ❧ ————————

Beneath the sandy earth, within the eggshells of an undetected nest, six spotted turtles have been growing steadily. The heat of July and August penetrated into the nest chamber by day and lingered there by night. Rains have come at propitious intervals, and in moist warmth the tiny turtles have prospered. As the end of August approaches, they are nearing the time to leave their nest.

By this time, fledgling birds have long since flown on untried wings to meet their fates. Those larvae and tadpoles that survived predation and early summer drought to wriggle or hop into damp and shady woodland recesses are now tiny hunters in shadows and darkness: spotted salamanders, peep frogs, wood frogs, and eastern gray tree frogs. Young pickerel frogs have begun to pursue crickets and grasshoppers in dew-soaked fields of seeding grass and flowering goldenrod, and miniature toads are venturing onto open sand. A second brood of song sparrows flutters through the swale, feeding on ripened seeds of reedgrass and numberless insects. For two months no killdeer cry has sounded over the nesting fields. While life moved

Mermaid weed, *Proserpinaca sp.*

along in the season passing over-head, the baby spotted turtles have been held in place, each in his own egg, together in the nest chamber.

The female spotted turtle became even more secretive dur-ing the days immediately following the raccoon's attack. Plants arched heavily over the water in the marsh, bent with the weight of seeds and fruits and the weariness of a full season's growth. The tur-tle could prowl about beneath these sheltering branches and leaves, along channels and musk-rat trails, in dark pools completely overgrown with buttonbush. For long periods of time she would burrow into crevices of mud and roots and be still. As waters lowered during the rainless early weeks of August, she withdrew once more into a safe and secret place, in a dark, wet hollow under a bank, and let the sunlit world go on above. Her nesting was long behind her now, and a longer sleep than this would pass before she nested again. There was no way to know if the eggs she buried in the earth in early June would survive to hatch into tur-tles, just as she could not know the fates of her nests of six

previous seasons.

The final week of August fades, late summer hints at autumn with rose and purple tinges in leaves and grass, and the time of hatch-ing draws near. With eyes that are ready for daylight, each turtle waits in darkness. Their carapaces are fully formed now, curved to fit the constraining contours of the sheltering eggshell. Although it will be years before their shells are large and strong enough to ward off teeth and claws, the turtles will be able to withdraw their heads, legs, and tails inside them even at hatching.

The turtles have become restless within their eggs. At the end of the first week of September, a baby turtle in the topmost egg scratches at the inner shell mem-branes. Soft sheaths that covered her claws, the sharp edges of her carapace, and the eggtooth just below her nose have been shed. The exposed cutting points begin to tear at the eggshell. The turtle's vigorous scratchings and head thrusts open a tiny slit in the end of her egg. Throughout the day she continues to work at the tough shell that envelops her. At last her struggles open a long tear in the egg. Her head and forefeet press

into the surrounding earth. Once the eggshell is opened, the kicking turtle pushes it away, loosening its constricting hold and freeing her carapace to begin to unfold from its tight oval. The yolk-sac that has nourished her growth through the long incubation in the earth will now fuel her first days, or even weeks, of life.

The hatchling spotted turtle is not ready to leave the nest at the time of pipping from her eggshell. She lies within the open shell for several days; her siblings have worked their eggshells open and rest close around her in the dark egg chamber. At times, their rest-less feet work in the earth.

Heavy rains come. An evening chill descends upon the low nest-ing fields and marsh. Thunder and lightning accompany leaden masses of clouds that obscure the sky at dusk. Clouds stall, cold rains fall all night long and through the next day. It is already to the nest-bound turtles' advan-tage that they are able to hold their breath. The deluge cannot be drained away quickly enough, and at times water fills the egg chamber and lies across the field. The turtles ride out the storm. As the rain slackens, water filters

away into deep sand beneath the nest, and air sifts into the earth. Close to emergence, and active within the confines of their nesting chamber, the turtles receive the oxygen they need.

September rains depart, and summer warmth returns. Not knowing the dazzling sunlight she is striving for, the hatchling turtle begins to dig upward. Six turtles begin to make their moves toward the open world. First, they must reach the surface of the earth that has cradled them for nearly three months; then they must make a crossing and find water they have never seen. Though she is only a little over an inch long, the hatchling spotted turtle is strong as she tunnels through the damp, resistant earth, and her legs work ceaselessly. The sandy soil grows warmer as she makes her inch-and-a-half journey to the surface.

After a few final clawings, earth loosens and crumbles away from her face. Her nostrils reach the open air of early afternoon. The turtle lies still, breathing. She forces her head outward, and light registers in her closed eyes. She blinks away the dirt. Her eyes open to take in the near blinding light of the earth's surface and a great blue vault extending to infinity over her head. She pauses, as if dazed by the world that has opened up before her. Her dark eyes read the light, the surface of the land, the shapes of distant trees. Messages of millions of years move through her. She thrusts forward and emerges on the flat sand. Long blue-green stems arc into the air above her, the brilliant yellow of goldenrod shimmers against the deep sky. She scrambles forward rapidly on a low carpet of moss that is soft and brilliant green after the rains.

Here she pauses again and continues her searching of the world around her, slowly craning her neck, shifting her head. She makes a quick run to the base of a clump of bluestem, stops

A sedge, *Carex crinita*.

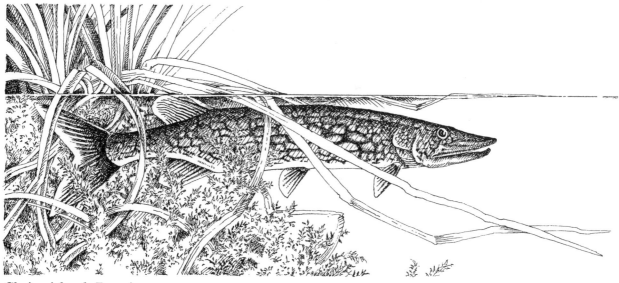

Chain pickerel, *Esox niger.*

in midstep, and reads the sky at the horizon once more. Her head is less than an inch above the ground. She cannot see the water of the marsh, which is nearly one hundred fifty yards distant and surrounded by tall growth. But she knows where the sheltering water lies. She sets off at a quick pace, climbing over the ridges of a deer's deep footprint in the sand.

There can be no stopping now. Some of the giant crickets singing from under bits of bark or in the shadows of the grass are bigger than she is. A small bird, a large toad, a young snake, almost any of the field's hunters could swallow her. She moves quickly, but she could not outrun a toad. Her only course is to reach the water, to go into hiding at once. She does not look back to see another hatchling blinking in the brilliant afternoon light.

With hot sun on her black shell and the warm earth beneath her, the hatchling travels rapidly. In less than half an hour she reaches the deep moss laced with winding strands of swamp blackberry that mark the beginning of the land's descent to the wet borders of the marsh. The flickering blackberry leaves and diminutive grasses in the moss provide some cover, but the turtle hurries on into the deep shadows of meadowsweet and steeplebush. The open field disappears behind her. She may not see it again for a decade, when she wanders out at dusk one evening late in spring to seek a site for her own first nest. Perhaps the great, great grandchildren of the deer whose tracks she crossed will be in their prime then and will see the light reflecting from her shell as she comes out into fields where they are feeding.

Patterns of dark leaves close out the dazzling September sky as the turtle makes her way over the wet sphagnum beneath dense shrubs. Dangers lurk in this deep shade as well as in the open field. Large frogs lie in wait, and snakes prowl the wet earth and the intertwining branches above it. But little has been astir in the midafternoon heat and stillness; the turtle's journey has gone unnoticed, and now she is at the edge of a space of open water, a small pool with soft rush and woolgrass towering above it. She slides into the shallows and makes a dive. This is the first time she has been immersed in her life, yet water is a familiar element. She begins to live as a turtle of the marsh now, hiding among the aquatic plants, slowly raising her head to the surface, taking a breath with just her nostrils above the water, then reaching her black head, with its scattering of yellow spots and streaks of orange at the sides, into the open air.

A creature of the sun, the turtle gradually makes her way beyond the shadows of the sedge. The surface here is scattered with the oval leaves of watershield and the dense growth that reaches from the surface to the shallow bottom.

She edges into the afternoon sun lying across the marsh. The sun and its seasons will mark her life, but for now she must remain hidden and take her sun through a thin veil of plants. Pickerel are poised like lances throughout the weedy shallows, and young bass move under the cover of lily pads. Herons stalk the sedges. The turtle will keep to water only a few inches deep and will not risk movement on the surface. She makes a space in the mossy water growth just beneath the surface, with an opening through which she can poke her nostrils for an occasional breath or reach her head above the water to look about from time to time. At any movement, any passing shadow, she pulls in quickly and lies in motionless concealment.

Shadows lengthen across the water, silhouettes of pine trees creep over waterlily islands, the sun slips into mist on the western horizon . . . night falls over the marsh. Stars emerge and glimmer on the water. As the night wears on, the Big Dipper shifts slightly toward its winter position.

Early the next morning, the last wisps of fog rise from the marsh and drift away on warming air, allowing sunlight into the water.

The hatchling awakens to water filled with light and lifts her head into the morning above the marsh. She is still hidden in the plants at the surface, which had been her bed. Already she is drawn to the sun. When it strengthens with the morning's passage, she crawls up among dried rushes, which are filled with warmth. She basks in their cover and feels the touch of the sun penetrating into her hiding place. When she slips back into the water, she finds towers and tunnels in weightless growth. She moves among shadows and lights in submarine pathways, pushing her head into the dense plants, disturbing small forms that dart and wriggle about her. Her eyes single out a tiny shape and focus; she thrusts her head out quickly, snapping up a bit of the life that teems in the water weeds. She pursues and overtakes an escaping larva; then, at the passing of a shadow, she turns and dives suddenly, kicking strongly into a hiding place on the bottom of her inches-deep pond. Motionless, without breathing, she waits a long time. When she feels that danger has passed, she will move again through the plants and water of her world.

Chapter Six

HIBERNATION

*Mi corazón espera también, hacía la luz y hacía la vida
otro milagro de la primavera.*

—Antonio Machado

30 September, 11 AM. *A hot September day, in the 80's; a few dancing breezes pick up as the hours pass . . . soft blue sky, hazy on the horizon, blurred drifts of small, scattered clouds. For a brief time at least, summer retakes the heavens, though the colors in the landscape cannot go unnoticed.*

Six screened-over nests remain here in the Digs, and I will continue to make daily checks of them until the ground begins to freeze. Most likely, any hatchlings in them are bound for overwintering in the nest, in which case I will leave them untouched and see what fate awaits them next spring. I do not think the placement of screens over the site, moments after the nesting mother left, could influence whatever is to happen with the turtles in the eggs beneath, so any observations I am able to make will constitute valuable field data.

When I dug into the nests I had transferred to my back fields, I found baby painted turtles waiting within, except for one nest in which none of the eggs had developed. Fully pipped, huddled as close together as their eggs had been, perfect little turtles lay in the earth, awaiting some message other than the intrusion of my carefully digging fingers. Some were still encased in their eggshells, with head and feet right at the doorway. Each was ready to leave on a moment's notice, each capable of digging out quickly and scrambling to the marsh, as soon as he was beckoned.

How incredible it seems that the hatchlings remaining in their nests out here in the Digs, completely developed, could sit quietly in the earth all these sun-filled days of late August and September and not be compelled to stir forth. In silence and darkness they will wait, as the warmth slowly leaves the earth surrounding them. Cold nights, chill rains, then cold days and nights together will slow down the metabolism of these unmoving turtles, and their weeks-long sleep of warmth will slip into a months-long sleep of cold. The ground will freeze around them and hold them in place as though they were encased in iron. Unless the coming winter conditions are unduly harsh, they will survive this, seed-like, until they are on the other side of the season of ice, when the call will finally come, and they will venture forth with the earth's springtime melting.

3 October, late afternoon. *Following two days of Indian-summer warmth and late afternoon mists that quieted the blazing color of the Virginia creeper and even quieted the song of crickets, a sharp drop in temperature has come. I return in the failing light to walk the nesting fields and check the covered nests, as I have every day since mid-August, even*

Rose hips of the swamp rose.

*though I am now certain I will
see no hatching. The little ones I
returned to the marsh last month
had a mild introduction to their
life in the wild, which will not
always be so benign.*

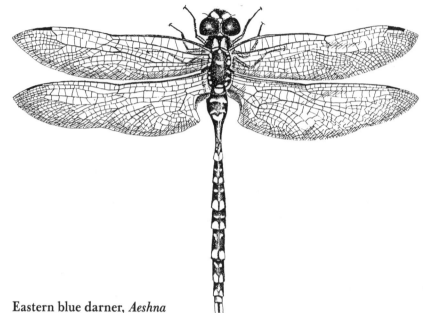

Eastern blue darner, *Aeshna
verticalis.*

S tiff, chilling breezes chase ripples across the channel below
the bridge. Eastern blue darners
still wheel in the open air above
the river, out over Blanding's
Marsh upstream, over the channel
and its low buttonbush, sedge,
and sweetgale margins downstream. These magnificent flyers
are the swallows of autumn, rising
high into the air, hovering in
place, or sweeping across the surface of the water, never resting.
They have survived some nights of
hard frost to fly these final days
over the marsh; unlike the departed swallows, they cannot escape the coming cold and can
only soar these mild afternoons
until their wings work no more.
They have left next year's dragonflies behind in countless eggs
deposited by aerial gymnastics all
over the wetlands. Perhaps the
ancestral turtle Proganochelys
would recognize the dragonfly,
whose own ancestors, on wings

two and a half feet wide, soared
over swamps that for millions of
years awaited the first turtle.

Though the dragonflies have
survived the first burning touches
of frost, the ferns have not. Ap-
propriate to its name, the sensitive
fern was the first to go, curling
away beneath alders that were still
green. Other ferns followed, bow-
ing in rich earth tones and sweet
scents of the ending season, dying
back in their own ancient ways to
await another season, which their
unfurling has come to symbolize.

The great thinning-out has begun,
especially in the buttonbush, sweetgale, and winterberry holly and
the alders that stand in the water.
And as they thin out, their leaves
fall to the surface of the water
they once hid from above, covering it even more closely, hiding
the turtles and anything else beneath
it all the more. Buttonbush, almost
leafless but still bearing its large
namesake spheres of seeds, shivers
in the wind. I miss the wet warm
mists of late yesterday afternoon.

The birds become furtive again

as autumn approaches. With the waning of summer they keep to shadows, grass tangles, and thickets; they are quick to take flight, and when they call to one another, it is in a whisper. The woodcocks are still here; I see the holes they bore each day in the mud of wet groves of willow, aspen, and alder. But they, too, are invisible now, not the conspicuous whirling dervishes that welcome spring.

Spent from its season of rampant growth, the reedgrass has begun to lie down in weary drifts throughout the Swale. It is hay that frost will mow and snow will bale. Its haylike scent already rises on updrafts of evening air from the hollow that six months ago smelled of thaw and mingles with the autumn aroma out of alder thickets, the scents of the wetland's final harvest.

Along the logging road, and here and there among the bluestem and sweetfern stands of the nesting fields, small white asters replace the burnt-out gray goldenrod. These diminutive asters, with their tiny-petalled white flowers, are similar in habit to the gray goldenrod, whose brilliant yellow shepherd staffs first dulled to umber gold and finally became an

earthen brown, which seems to disappear in the landscape. Just out from the tree line, bordering the fields and only a few feet from some of the painted turtles' favorite nesting places, are drifts of blue, the blue of smooth aster, which seems the same in sunlight or in shadow. A scattering of autumn leaves has blown out onto the open sand and moss, and some have caught in the screens covering the turtle nests.

All is quiet. Yet one never knows about these turtles. I once went out to paint a watercolor of reedgrass and water during the second week of October, when I had thought that all turtle activity had been concluded for the season, and found two hatchling snapping turtles lying among the cranberry vines below the marsh in which I was going to paint. Trees were all but leafless, a flock of geese flew high overhead, yet these little turtles, seemingly out of season, were seeking their place in the world. I need to be here to lift the covering screen, should any of the hatchlings act on a last-minute message to leave the nest.

A farewell gathering of blackbirds raises a loud, sustained clamor among the topmost branches

of tall pines above the Great Swale. After their strong spring presence, these birds fade into far corners of the landscape and seem not to exist until their raucous autumn regatherings. They are like the killdeer, so noisily present and so conspicuous a part of every early-season day (and night, in the case of the killdeer) that it seems they will be there forever. I am never aware of their departure and cannot pinpoint the day; I

Bur-reed, *Sparganium sp.*

Hatchling snapping turtle among cranberry vines.

just suddenly realize that they are gone. I inspect the covered nest at the edge of the hayfield and the far one by the clear-cut. All are waiting still. I walk down to the pool below the clear-cut, where I released some hatchlings. Breezes shiver through the bur-reed. Somewhere in this little landscape, baby turtles are hiding.

In the hayfield, the striking purple panicles of the witch grass have been bleached to straw. A few of these have broken loose already and roll and tumble across the bright green plain flecked with flame-red leaves of sorrel. Moving back into the nesting fields, I take a last look along the rim of the big sandpit, where I saw a nestful of snapping turtles dig out of the sand. The low sun catches in the silken tufts that line the seeding stalks of the bluestem, lighting a silvery sheen above the sand. A marsh hawk wings low over the field without noticing me as I stand still in the shadows at the lower end of the sandpit. She sweeps over the mossy ground where bluets grew in spring, circles the cranberry hollows and brush of the deer thicket, and then wings off toward the Great Swale.

With the marsh hawk's departure, I take my own leave. In the distance, a peep frog calls. At the end of a mild day in autumn, one of these singers of spring will sometimes raise a solitary song, perhaps remembering April, perhaps bidding the season farewell.

18 October, late afternoon. *Hot, nearly 80, but it is not summer. Even if I close my eyes so that I cannot see the long shadows and leafless trees or the sere colors that have come over the marsh, I can feel that the heat comes from an autumn sun, a sun too low on the horizon to stay the season's progress. Color remains in the foliage on the water — the reds, maroons, purples, and rare splashes of gold or green of the watershield. Purple deepens to black in the lily pads, most of which have sunk beneath the surface and begun to disintegrate. This is probably my last wading of the year — the heat of this day can do nothing to reverse the cold that has steadily penetrated the water of the Great Marsh. Light winds stirring, grasses and sedges swaying . . . high, widely spaced puffs of cloud drift by, all riding the same upper level of air.*

I wade into the shallows of the cove, hoping to see a spotted turtle one last time this season that is so close to its final day, but I have no such luck. They may be out somewhere in the waterways of the Digs, but I am not in the right place. I remember the sun of past Octobers glowing on the shells of somnolent spotted turtles who had wedged themselves among cranberry vines to take their last basking of the year, and I think back to a woodland brook where beneath a float of autumn leaves a brilliant turtle had paused in the midst of some autumn migration. Perhaps I have walked by one here, hidden in sunlit sedges or lying beneath tangles of the last water plants and swirls of leaves that have blown this far out over the marsh. Or perhaps they are all on their way to spring, asleep beneath the water and mud.

Painted turtles yet cruise the chill water . . . an adventurous hatchling is on the move. The big ones seem immobile. I stand still for half an hour or so, as the afternoon fades, for my last immersed look at the marsh. There are six painted turtles who do not move the entire time. All but one face the same direction, pretty much due south. The nonconformist faces the exact opposite direction, lest I come to any fanciful, but erroneous, conclusions. The light catches in a white point in each turtle's eye and where the water touches each head. They are as static as if they were literally painted turtles, each decorated with two glints of silver gilt; lemon-gold would serve for the stripes on their black heads and the spot behind each eye. The sun lies low across the marsh, lighting these daydreaming turtles perfectly and illuminating the gold-ringed eyes and yellow throats of two young male bullfrogs sitting near me in the water.

When one of the clouds passes over the sun, there is an immediate, sharply perceptible loss of heat . . . the light, color, and life all seem to fade from the scene before me; the glowing gold and green of the bullfrogs, the brilliant head markings and eye gleams of the turtles all go out, like lights extinguished. It is time to wade from the marsh. I move; the turtles withdraw their heads; frogs watch, immobile, as I depart. With stiffened feet and ankles, I walk out onto dry land and look back across the Great Marsh. In the deep expanse above it, a large cloud formation has taken on a surreal and recognizable shape. It is Archelon, and the sky, for a moment, is the sea of one hundred million years ago.

Days shorten. The sun arcs lower in the sky each afternoon.

Marsh hawk, *Circus cyaneus*.

Water in the marsh and its surrounding wetlands loses heat on frosted nights that cannot be regained even on the most brilliant days. The turtles slow with the season, even though autumnbasking in sheltered places grants them moments of near-summer life. The sun's hold on the earth weakens; heat in the air and water diminishes. There is little for the turtles to draw from.

As their ambient temperatures drop at the end of their season, turtles are faced with the matter of hibernation. The physiology of a hibernating mammal, such as a groundhog, is different from that of a hibernating turtle. Mammals operate on a sort of biological time clock, which is not strictly tied to external temperatures. When these animals enter hibernation, internal adjustments take their body temperature close to 40°F., and hold it there. Mammalian metabolism becomes regulated at this low temperature, and a major metabolic surge is needed to bring the animal quickly out of hibernation. This is provided in large measure by rapid oxidation of brown fat, accumulated during the summer and fall, which generates tremendous energy within the mammal. A turtle's (or any other ectotherm's) endurance of and emergence from the deep, prolonged torpor of winter is accompanied by quite different, but equally profound, metabolic adjustments.

Hibernation is a difficult aspect of turtle behavior for researchers to investigate. Environmental conditions and the extreme inaccessibility of the turtles—under thick ice, icy water, and mud—make it hard to find out just what is happening in the wild during this remarkable part of a turtle's life. Field observation and experiments with radio tracking devices, and work with laboratory experiments under simulated natural conditions have provided a few insights, however, into an impressive survival story.

Except for hatchlings overwintering in the nest, all turtles must find a place to hibernate. Painted turtles dive to the bottom of ponds or lakes, in water depths of up to three feet, but generally shallower, and usually burrow into soft mud. It is possible that they shift deeper into the mud during hibernation, to gain a degree or two of heat. The mud is always warmer than the water above it and is increasingly warmer at greater depths. Painted turtles have been known to hibernate nearly a foot and a half into the mud of a pond bottom, where the temperature could be as much as 4°F. higher than it is where mud meets water. Under a mantle of ice, the water temperature at a depth of a foot or so might be in the range of 38°F.; four inches into the mud the temperature might be close to 40°F.; and at a foot and a half it could be as high as 42°F.

It is perhaps misleading to speak of warmth; a few degrees would seem to matter little. But these few degrees can mean the difference between life and death to a hibernating turtle. Essentially, a turtle must keep from freezing and yet stay cold enough to maintain a metabolic depression that will enable him to survive for up to six months without drawing a breath. The turtle must pass the same span of time without eating; however, at temperatures only several degrees above freezing, energy requirements are close enough to zero that hibernating turtles experience little if any weight loss.

The primary stress of hibernation comes from an extremely restricted access to oxygen and the resultant buildup of lactic acid. This is particularly acute in species such as the painted turtle, who bury themselves in the underwater mud—which is an anaerobic environment below a depth of as little as an eighth of an inch. Under mantles of ice and snow, water itself often becomes oxygen-depleted, and even fish, with their water-breathing gills, will perish. Painted turtles have a variety of unique and complicated metabolic strategies that allow them to function as anaerobes, however. (And painted turtles, among others, are able to draw calcium carbonate from their shells as a buffer for acidosis, somewhat as one might use limestone to help neutralize acidic garden conditions.)

All turtle species are able to absorb oxygen directly from and release carbon dioxide directly to the water by way of blood vessels in their skin, throat lining, or cloaca. This enables them to go for long periods of time without coming to the surface for air breathing. Softshell turtles are especially efficient at this type of nonpulmonary respiration; they are even capable of taking oxygen from the water via networks of capillaries close to the surface of the undersides of their leathery carapaces. Musk turtles are also efficient at underwater gas exchanges and can function as water breathers at low temperatures. They have been known to survive five months without access to air in aerated water at a temperature of about 38°F.

Painted turtles are able to absorb some oxygen from water, and it is possible that during hibernation they are able to move out of the mud and into the water, or at least extend their heads into the water, to take up amounts of oxygen that would help to ameli-

orate the great stress of hibernation. Turtles with the greatest
capacity for underwater gas exchange, however, exhibit the least
tolerance for oxygen deprivation
and would appear likely to seek
hibernacula with access to oxygenated water, rather than to bury
themselves in the mud. It is
possible that species possessing
high extrapulmonary respiration
capabilities, such as the musk and
softshell turtles, alternate periods
of burrowing into the bottom with
exposure to oxygenated water over
the course of hibernation.

Some turtles pass the first
winter of their lives in the nest. In
the northernmost reaches of their
range, painted turtles rarely dig
out in autumn, but overwinter in
the nest as fully developed hatchlings. A six-year monitoring of
painted-turtle nests in Ontario,
Canada, revealed no instances of
hatchling emergence in the fall.
These hatchling painted turtles
have been found to have freeze
tolerance, which enables them to
survive repeated exposures to temperatures as low as 18°F. and the
freezing of as much as fifty-three
percent of their body water. Conditions beyond these points are
fatal. For periods of days, or even

weeks, when the temperature in
their nest dips below freezing, the
baby turtles stop breathing, their
hearts stop beating, and their
blood ceases flowing.

The capacity to withstand freezing at any stage has been demon-
strated only for five other vertebrates—young garter snakes and
four species of frogs that hibernate
on land. But for most turtle
species, it appears that freezing is
lethal—even for hatchlings. This is
the case with snapping turtles,
who must dig out of their nests
before winter sets in, unless they
are in a location where the temperature in the nest never drops
below freezing. Success in autumn-
hatching in areas of short summers, or in hatchling overwintering in the nest, may be factors
that determine the northern range
limits of turtle species. Many
species of turtles do successfully
overwinter in the nest, but most of
these appear to represent freeze
avoidance rather than freeze
tolerance: they inhabit areas
where the scant layer of earth
above them provides sufficient in-
sulation to keep the temperature
in the nest above 32°F. through
most winters. In cases where the
temperature falls below freezing,

the nests fail.

Snow cover is essential for
winter survival of hatchling turtles—even for freeze-tolerant
hatchling painted turtles. An entire population's hatchlings may be
lost in the nest if there is insuffi-
cient snow cover to protect them
from winter extremes. With such
protection, the air temperature
may drop as low as −16°F. without the nest temperature falling
below 20°F., which is within the
survival margin of the baby
turtles. Snow has such a capacity
for insulating that beneath its
drifts temperatures in a turtle nest
rarely fall below 30°F.

Adult turtles must find overwintering sites in which they can
avoid freezing. Although instances
of eastern box turtles burying
themselves in mud at the bottom
of a pond or stream have been
reported, they nearly always hibernate on land. Sometimes they make
use of mammal burrows, and, on
occasion, several will share a
hibernaculum. Box turtles dig
deeper into earth as winter pro-
gresses and may end up as far as
two feet below the surface. Other
species overwinter beneath the
water, usually in the bottom mud.

After a summer of wandering in

pine groves, wooded thickets, and grassy fields, wood turtles return to pools in permanent streams, or to slow-moving rivers, to pass the winter under water, at depths of about three feet. Some bury themselves in soft bottom mud to depths of up to a foot; others rest on the bottom or wedge themselves under banks, among tree roots and rocks beneath the water.

Over much of their range spotted turtles pass the winter beneath as little as four to ten inches of water, burrowing into mud from about five to ten inches. Those that I have observed in the North, however, emerge in situations where the water is sixteen to eighteen inches deep and generally where there is a slight current.

These factors may be of importance in preventing ice from reaching the bottom and penetrating the mucky substrate. I have been surprised to find snapping turtles emerging from hibernation in locations similar to and quite close to those selected by spotted turtles. Snappers may use combinations of shallow water and deep mud even in the North and often hibernate near an inlet stream or other site where the water is likely to be aerated. It is possible that they rely on extending their long necks out of the mud so that they are able to extract oxygen from water pumped in and out of their mouth and throat.

It appears that some turtles return year after year to a desirable hibernation niche within their home range, just as they do to favorable foraging and nesting areas. In three successive seasons I found the same recently emerged male spotted turtle within a one-hundred-foot stretch of a small tussock-sedge marsh; on two occasions, the marsh was still almost completely frozen over. I have never found another emerging spotted turtle in the same marsh, nor have I found that male there at other times of the year. It would seem to represent his winter quarters, and for whatever reason, he appears to have it to himself. I have made two captures of an emergent female spotted turtle in a flooded alder thicket, the second coming one year, one day, and one hour after the first, in a spot about five feet from the first finding. Other species may demonstrate fidelity to a safe hibernaculum as well. I have found the same Blanding's turtle, under ice, at the first thaw of two consecutive springs, at points separated by less than four feet; and I have seen painted turtles reappear in the same small areas year after year.

Just as turtles cannot miss their cues to hibernate, they must know when spring has come. According-

Wood turtle, *Clemmys insculpta.*

Canada goose, *Branta canadensis.*

ly, they spend the winter beneath comparatively shallow water, where the first signals of the warming season will reach them. In autumn they seek out places that meet their needs for winter survival and that will be among the earliest to thaw. This is of special importance to the turtles of the North, who have little time to spare for the mating, nesting, and hatching activities essential to the turtle season. When the ice mantle melts away at last, and springtime enters the water, the turtles

begin to stir. They may sense a change in temperature as slight as three or four degrees and respond to the turning season. Even hibernating turtles, seemingly insensate, are in intimate touch with the elements of the earth they have inhabited for such a long time.

27 October. *Late October, it could be November. Slate-gray day, near 40 degrees, it is probably close to a good hibernation temperature in the mud, water, and sky alike on a day like this. The wind's con-*

stant rustle in the reedgrass sounds like something on the move this time of year, something more tangibly alive than wind, more substantive than the spirits of the departing season.

Suddenly a strange sound fills the air, a loud buzzing drone, like the deep whistling of some gigantic arrow; it is loud enough to make me think of an airplane. A solitary Canada goose slices out of the wind, low over the leafless thicket in which I stand, passes directly over my head in a high-speed descent, and disappears far out among the leatherleaf islands in the marsh. I hear the landing I cannot see. The startling passage of this bird, his long neck fully extended, his wings held down, stiff and unmoving, flight feathers flared out, took place in an instant. I marvel at the strength in the descending bird, the force and dynamics he achieves in the medium of thin air. I can imagine the braking impact of his landing in the water, and I can better imagine those long, high migration flights, taken by day and by night.

My back to the stiffening wind, I look over the marsh. The water is clear now around the bordering rushes and sedges. These will persevere even through the snow and ice to come. Watery growth has died away, and I can look into the depths more clearly, now that there are no turtles to see. Despite the season, I still expect to see some last shifting of a turtle's shell.

My eyes return to a search of the shallows. No turtles move. They have been seen swimming under ice at times, but it cannot be a favorite pastime with them. These frigid excursions seem to occur at the last possible moments preceding hibernation or the first ones following it. Even in midwinter there may be occasional secret shiftings under the cover of ice and snow, for reasons known only to the turtles.

But the year of the turtle is over. A time of deepening stillness settles over the marsh. Sleep and silence will be the rule. I turn from the cold, black waters of the marsh. It will be a long time now until clear snowmelt runs over gravel and the cries of the killdeer break winter's silence. I walk out the logging road and leave the marsh to the deer and the winter birds, the northwest wind and the snow. As I lean my walking stick against the stone gatepost, I look for the trust and the patience of the turtles, and await the thaw.

———————— ⌀ ————————

The spotted turtle moves against the current of a shallow stream that winds through alders and red maples. This woodland brook is more open now; the trees are thinned out as leaves fade and fall, swirling along the banks, gathering in root crevices, and blanketing the black waters of still pools beyond the reach of the current. On the dark stream bottom the turtle is invisible but for her pattern of yellow spots and the orange markings along the sides of her head, which glow in the dark water as she passes under openings in the mats of leaves. These islands turning slowly on the surface of the stream flash brilliantly with the fall colors of red-maple leaves and alder leaves.

Passing in and out of shafts of sunlight, sliding under the mats of leaves, the turtle swims along the bottom of the brook, following its winding course through a wet woodland she has traversed during other seasons of her life. At times she turns close against the bank, sets her feet, and slowly reaches her head out of the water. She rests and breathes, and surveys the land around her.

At a familiar point she leaves the water, climbs a mossy bank among the alder roots, and sets off through a little wood, rustling in the fallen leaves. She makes her way to a slight rise of land and ascends to a quieter ridge of deep rust-colored needles under a stand of white pine. She crawls on through a border of aspen and birch seedlings, then passes under

a miniature forest of bracken fern, gold and glowing brown, curled like clenched fists after the burn of the first hard frosts but still standing on wine-red stems. Creamy, gray-green aspen bark reflects the autumn light. The final trembling leaves of quaking aspen, deep green splashed with clear gold, flutter and whisper in the slight October breeze. The turtle comes to the dry moss borders of the sandy nesting fields, not far from where she dug her nest far back in the season.

Shadows are long now. Even a little past midday they extend from tall pines on the edge of the field away out across its plane, giving a late-in-the-day feeling to early afternoon. The ground cools quickly in the shade; there is little warmth for the turtle to pick up if she lowers herself to rest. But autumn warmth lingers in the air, and her dark shell has taken heat from the sun during her overland passage. She continues rapidly on her way, crossing beds of moss that have revived in autumn rain and morning mists and are now embellished with clusters of pale yellow and rose mushrooms.

Her journey has an immediacy. She comes out onto the open field and crosses it without a pause. She passes through the sweetfern colony, only a yard or two from a small hole in the earth at the base of one of the plants. In an earthen cavity beneath the exit hole, a few inches deep, lie the shell fragments left behind by her six hatchlings.

Once across the open sand she crawls over the moss and short grass tufts at the edge of the field. She passes many small excavations with scattered bits of dried egg-shells lying next to them and works her way among the inter-twined strands of dewberry vines with shiny black-purple leaves. She enters the tall dense grass of the slope leading to the water. Bleached and glowing softly in the sun, a forest of sedge arches above her. A few brilliant red leaves re-main on blueberry stems to blaze among the pale grasses. She comes onto wet moss carpets, chill in the shade and the cooling waters of the wetlands, and makes her way around and through dense clumps of grass and Canada rush, where she sinks into the water. Even late in the season, there is no open water in the alder thickets of the swale.

The turtle makes her way through the tangles beneath the

surface, passing through watery tunnels with woven walls of thousands of plant stems. A short distance from the boggy sphagnum, she turns and follows the contours of the water zone. She has a knowledge of the water's nebulous geography, an awareness of the autumn light beneath the silvery surface.

The spotted turtle surfaces once and looks around. Light from the low-lying sun glows in white pines on a ridge above the swamplands. It is not a summer light. The chilling breeze of ending day that vibrates stiff sedges in the water around her is not a summer breeze. The season is gone. Life is withdrawing, slowing down, sleeping, or dying away. She cannot hear the distant wild calling of the geese or see their long columns, mere specks in the deep October sky. As they make their journey of thousands of miles, the turtle draws her head beneath the water and makes her descent of less than two feet. She will find a place, draw her life deep within herself, and wait out the coming and going of the ice.

The turtle has breathed her last breath of the season and will not see open air again until the dawning of another spring, a dawning that lies on the far side of winter. Her movements slow in the cold water. She arches her head and investigates the muck bottom, the water's winding route among the alders and fern mounds, muskrat paths and fallen logs. She enters a watery thicket of alder and buttonbush and noses among its roots. For a number of autumns she has returned to this same area to seek her hibernaculum. Closing her eyes, she digs and feels her way into mud and roots, lodging herself firmly in place. The ice will not reach her here. She settles into her half year of stillness.

Autumn colors burn out around the marsh. Maroon gives way to black as the last lily pads sink beneath wind-riffled waters. The final calls of disappearing sparrows fade among dogwood and alders. Geese trumpet in from the early twilight sky and rest on the leaden water. When the last of them departs, the marsh is left to silence, wind, and the notes of winter birds.

Chill deepens in the water. Ice closes up the marsh. Mounting layers of snow silently cover the ice. Night after night in the harshest depth of winter, as Orion and the Pleiades burn distant and brilliant in the black sky and strong winds howl off the mountain to the northwest, the turtles rest beneath the ice. With the life in them nearly suspended, reduced to its most tenuous hold, all but extinct in the vast, inhospitable regime that reaches above them to the limits of the universe, they lie within their shells, waiting for the earth to make its required turnings and return them to the sun that will awaken them to another season. ❦

CAPTIONS FOR COLOR PLATES

Between pages 16 & 17: **Spotted turtles basking.**

Between pages 32 & 33: **Wood turtle in a stream.**

Between pages 48 & 49: **Spotted turtles in a courtship chase.**

Between pages 80 & 81: **Spotted turtle nesting in moonlight.**

Between pages 112 & 113: **Young eastern painted turtle basking among white waterlilies.**

Between pages 128 & 129: **Spotted turtle hatchling.**

Between pages 144 & 145: **Spotted turtle and watershield.**

Between pages 160 & 161: **Hibernating spotted turtle.**

Pondweed, *Potamogetan sp.*

SELECTED BIBLIOGRAPHY

Alexander, M. R. (1943). Snapping turtle food. *Journal of Wildlife Management* 7 (3):279–282.

Babcock, H. L. (1919). The turtles of New England. *Memoirs of the Boston Society of Natural History* 8 (3):325–431. Reprinted by Dover Press as *Turtles of the Northeastern United States*. (1971), New York.

Bennett, D. H., Gibbons, J. W., and Franson, J. C. (1970). Terrestrial activity in aquatic turtles. *Ecology* 51: 738–740.

Breitenbach, G. L., Congdon, J. D., and Van Loben Sels, R. C. (1984). Winter temperatures of *Chrysemys picta* nests in Michigan: effects on hatchling survival. *Herpetologica* 40:79–81.

Burke, A. C. (1989). Critical features in chelonian development: the ontogeny of a unique tetrapod Bauplan. Ph.D. thesis. Harvard University, Cambridge, Massachusetts.

Bury, R. B. (1979). Review of the ecology and conservation of the bog turtle, *Clemmys muhlenbergi*. *United States Fish and Wildlife Service Special Science Report,* Wildlife No. 219.

Cagle, F. R. (1954). Observations on the life cycles of painted turtles (Genus *Chrysemys*). *American Midland Naturalist* 52 (1):225–235.

Carr, A. F. (1952). *Handbook of Turtles*. Comstock Publishing Associates, Cornell University Press, Ithaca, New York.

Congdon, J. D., Tinkle, D. W., Breitenbach, G. L., and Van Loben Sels, R. C. (1983). Nesting ecology and hatching success in the turtle *Emydoidea blandingi*. *Herpetologica* 39:417–429.

Ernst, C. H. (1971a). Population dynamics and activity cycles of *Chrysemys picta* in southeastern Pennsylvania. *Journal of Herpetology* 5:151–160.

——— (1972). Temperature–activity relationship in the painted turtle, *Chrysemys picta*. *Copeia,* 217–222.

——— (1975). Growth of the spotted turtle, *Clemmys guttata*. *Journal of Herpetology* 9:313–318.

——— (1976). Ecology of the spotted turtle, *Clemmys guttata* (Reptilia, Testudines, Testudinidae), in southeastern Pennsylvania. *Journal of Herpetology* 10:25–33.

——— (1977). Biological notes on the bog turtle, *Clemmys muhlenbergii*. *Herpetologica* 33:241–246.

——— (1982). Environmental temperatures and activities in wild spotted turtles, *Clemmys guttata*. *Journal of Herpetology* 16:112–120.

——— (1986a). Ecology of the turtle, *Sternotherus odoratus,* in southeastern Pennsylvania. *Journal of Herpetology* 20:341–352.

——— (1986b). Environmental temperatures and activities in the wood turtle, *Clemmys insculpta*. *Journal of Herpetology* 20:222–229.

Ernst, C. H. and Barbour, R. E. (1972). *Turtles of the United States*. University Press of Kentucky, Lexington.

Ewert, M. A. (1985). "Embryology of Turtles." In *Biology of the Reptilia*. Ed. by Gans, C. and Billet, F. John Wiley and Sons, New York.

Gibbons, J. W. (1968a). Reproductive potential, activity and

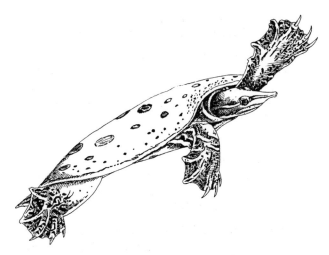

Eastern spiny softshell, *Trionyx s. spinifera.*

cycles in the painted turtle, *Chrysemys picta. Ecology* 49 (3):399–409.

——— (1986d). Observations on the ecology and population dynamics of the Blanding's turtle, *Emydoidea blandingi. Canadian Journal of Zoology* 46: 288–290.

Gibbons, J. W. and Nelson, D. H. (1978). The evolutionary significance of delayed emergence from the nest by hatchling turtles. *Evolution* 32:297–303.

Graham, T. E. and Doyle, T. S. (1977). Growth and population characteristics of the Blanding's turtle, *Emydoidea blandingii*, in Massachusetts. *Herpetologica* 33:410–414.

——— (1979). Dimorphism, courtship, eggs, and hatchlings of the Blanding's turtle, *Emydoidea blandingii*, in Massachusetts. *Journal of Herpetology* 13 (1): 125–127.

Halliday, T. and Adler, K. (eds.) (1986). *Encyclopedia of Reptiles and Amphibians.* Facts on File, New York.

Hammer, D. A. (1969). Parameters of a marsh snapping turtle population, LaCreek Refuge, South Dakota. *Journal of Wildlife Management* 33 (4):995–1005.

——— (1971). The durable snapping turtle. *Natural History.* 80 (6):58–65.

Harless, M. and Morlock, H. (eds.) (1979). *Turtles, Perspectives and Research.* John Wiley and Sons, New York.

Kiviat, E. (1980). A Hudson River tidemarsh snapping turtle population. *Proceedings Northeast Section, The Wildlife Society.* 37:158–168.

Linck, M. H., DePari, J. A., Butler, B. O., and Graham, T. E. (1989). Nesting behavior of the turtle *Emydoidea blandingi*, in Massachusetts. *Journal of Herpetology* 23:442–444.

MacCulloch, R. D. and Secoy, D. M. (1983). Demography, growth, and food of western painted turtles, *Chrysemys picta bellii* (Gray), from southern Saskatchewan. *Canadian Journal of Zoology* 61:1499–1509.

McLoughlin, J. (1981). "The Snapping Turtle." *Country Journal,* Vol. 8, No. 7, 30–34.

Obbard, M. E. and Brooks, R. J. (1981). Fate of overwintered clutches of the common snapping turtle, *Chelydra serpentina*, in Algonquin Park, Ontario. *Canadian Field-Naturalist* 95 (3):350–352.

Obst, F. J. (1986). *Turtles, Tortoises, and Terrapins.* St. Martin's Press, New York.

Packard, G. C., Packard, M. J., McDaniel, P. L., and McDaniel, L. L. (1989). Tolerance of hatchling painted turtles to subzero temperatures. *Canadian Journal of Zoology* 67:828–830.

Paukstis, G. L., Shuman, R. D., and Janzen, F. J. (1989).

Supercooling and freeze tolerance in hatchling painted turtles (*Chrysemys picta*). *Canadian Journal of Zoology* 67:1082–1084.

Peterson, C. C. (1987). Thermal regulation of hibernating painted turtles. *Journal of Herpetology.* 21 (1):16–20.

Pritchard, P. C. H. (1967). *Living Turtles of the World.* T.F.H. Publications, Inc., Jersey City, New Jersey.

Risley, P. L. (1933). Observations on the natural history of the common musk turtle, *Sternotherus odoratus* (Latreille). *Papers of the Michigan Academy of Science, Arts, and Letters.* 7:686–711.

Storey, K. B., Storey, J. M., Brooks, S. P. J., Churchill, T. A., and Brooks, R. J. (1988). Hatchling turtles survive freezing during winter hibernation. *Proceedings of the National Academy of Sciences, USA* 85:8350–8354.

Taylor, G. M. and Nol, E. (1989). Movements and hibernation sites of overwintering painted turtles in southern Ontario. *Canadian Journal of Zoology* 67:1877–1881.

Ultsch, G. R. (1989). Ecology and physiology of hibernation and overwintering among freshwater fishes, turtles and snakes. *Biological Review* 64:435–516.

Ultsch, G. R. and Jackson, D. C. (1982a). Long–term submergence at 3°C of the turtle *Chrysemys picta bellii* in normoxic and severely hypoxic water. I. Survival, gas exchange, and acid-base balance. *Journal of Experimental Biology* 97:11–28.

——— (1982b). Long–term submergence at 3°C of the turtle *Chrysemys picta bellii* in normoxic and severely hypoxic water. III. Effects of changes in ambient P_{O_2} and subsequent air-breathing. *Journal of Experimental Biology* 97:87–99.

Ultsch, G. R. and Lee, D. (1983). Radiotelemetric observations of wintering snapping turtles (*Chelydra serpentina*) in Rhode Island. *Journal of the Alabama Academy of Sciences* 54:200–206.

Ward, F. P., Hohmann, C. J., Ulrich, J. F., and Hill, S. E. (1976). Seasonal microhabitat selections of spotted turtles (*Clemmys guttata*) in Maryland elucidated by radioisotope tracking. *Herpetologica* 32:60–64.

INDEX

Page numbers in *italics* indicate illustrations appear on that page.

A

Acer rubrum. See Red maple
Aeshna verticalis. See Eastern blue
    darner
Agelaius phoeniceus. See Redwinged
    blackbird
Age of turtle, determining, 28
Aggression, and courtship and
    mating, 56
Alder, 67
    thicket, *33*
        map, 14-15
Alnus rugosa. See Alder
Ambystoma maculatum. See Spotted
    salamanders
American woodcock, *17*
Amnion, 81
Andropogon scoparius. See Bluestem
    grass
Aquatic insects, 20, 32, 41
Archelon, 26, 27
Ardea herodias. See Great blue heron
Aronia melanocarpa. See Black
    chokeberry
Asclepias incarnata. See Swamp
    milkweed
Asynchronous emergence, 135

Autumn emergence of hatchlings, 137

B

Basking, 34-36
    eastern painted turtles, *21*
    snapping turtle, 100, *101*
    spotted turtle, *38*, 102
Beaver dam, 19, *19*
Behavior
    basking, *21*, 34-36, *38*, 100, *101*, 102
    biting, 56-57
    courtship, 49-61
    defensive, 27-31
    emergence, 37-41
        of hatchling, 137-139
    feeding, 114-116
    fighting, 52-55, *53*
    hatchling, 137-139, 141-143
    hiding, 22, 35, 102
    hunting, 41, 114-115
    mating, 57-58, *57*, 61
    nesting, 56, 65, 76-80, 83, 87-89,
        88, 93-97, *95*
Biting, during courtship and mating,
    56-57
Black chokeberry, *63*
Black-crowned night heron, *64*
Blanding's turtle, *118*
    feeding, 115
    hibernation sites, 157

sexual maturity, 51
Blue-flag iris, *44, 120*
    seedpod, *128*
Bluestem grass, *130*
Bog turtle, *11*
    home range, 110
Box turtle
    basking, 36
    feeding, 115
    sense of homing, 110
    See also Eastern box turtle; Ornate
    box turtle
Branta canadensis. See Canada goose
Broad-leaved arrowhead, *105*
Bullfrog, *49*
Bur-reed, *151*
Buttonbush, *61*

C

Canada goose, *158*
Canada rush, *169*
Carapace
    evolution of, 25
    injuries to, 105
    scutes, *16, 80*
    snapping turtle, 23, *113*
Carex crinita. See Sedge
Cephalanthus occidentalis. See
    Buttonbush
Chain pickerel, *146*

Chamaedaphne calyculata. See Leatherleaf

Charadrius vociferus. See Killdeer

Chelonia. *See* Turtle; specific turtle breeds

Chelydra serpentina. See Snapping turtle

Chrysemys picta picta. See Eastern painted turtle

Cinnamon fern, *47*

Circus cyaneus. See Marsh hawk

Clemmys guttata. See Spotted turtle

Clemmys insculpta. See Wood turtle

Clemmys muhlenbergii. See Bog turtle

Cold-blooded. *See* Ectotherm

Coloration, 50-51

Comptonia peregrina. See Sweetfern

Courtship, 42-61
    behavior patterns, 56
    chase, 58, 59-61
    spotted turtle, 59-61
    time of year, 55

Cove, map, 14-15

Cranberry
    flower, *103*
    vines, *152*

Cryptodirans, 25

Cryptozooic tendencies of spotted turtles, 35, 102

D

Daily activity range. *See* Home range

Defensive behavior, 27-31

Diamondback terrapin, survival tactics, 55-56

Diet, 116-119

Digs, map, 14-15

Dormancy in summer, 102

Dytiscidae. See Predaceous diving beetle

E

Eastern blue darner, *150*

Eastern box turtle, *117*
    courtship, 56
    eye color, 51
    gender differences, 50
    hibernation sites, 156
    home range, 109
    longevity of, 51
    mating, 51
    survival tactics, 55-56
    See also Box turtle

Eastern painted turtle, *21. See also* Painted turtle

Eastern spiny softshell, *165*

Ectotherm, 35

Eggs, 66
    incubation, 81-82, 134
    location in nest, 80
    pipping, 134
    predation, 70-71, 96
    shape differences among species, 90
    shells, 82
    snapping turtle, 90

Embryonic development, 66, 81-82, 85, 112

Embryos, protection in nest, 134

Emergence
    from hibernation, 13-41
    of hatchlings, 137

Emydoidea blandingii. See Blanding's turtle

Ephemeroptera. See Mayflies

Epigaea repens. See Mayflowers

Esox niger. See Chain pickerel

Estivation, 102

Evolution
    reptilian embryo development, 81
    turtle, 24-27

Extinct turtle species, 26-27

Eye
    eastern box turtle, 51
    snapping turtle, *24*

F

False nest, 67

Feeding, 41, 114-116

Fertilization of eggs, 50, 137

Fighting, 27-31, 52-55

Floating-leaf pondweed, *115*

Food, 41

Fossil records, 25, 26

Freeze tolerance, 156

Frogs, 37, *49*

G

Gender development, and nest temperatures, 82

Gender differences among turtles, 50-51

Giant tortoises, courtship behavior, 56

Giant water bug, 20

Glyceria canadensis. See Rattlesnake

manna grass
Grackles, common, 32, *32*
Gray goldenrod, *131*
Great blue heron, *121*
Great Marsh, map, 14-15
Great Swale, *104*
 map, 14-15
Growth rings on plastron plates, 48

H

Hatching, 126-147
 description, 144-147
Hatchling
 behavior, 141-143
 development, 134
 emergence, 137-139
 snapping turtle, 131-134, *142, 152*
 spotted turtle, 129, 137-139, *139*
Hibernacula. *See* Hibernation, sites
Hibernation, 148-161
 effects of, 21
 painted turtles, 155-156
 sites, 36, 155-157
 stress, 155
 timing of, 157-158
"Hidden-necked" turtles, 25
Hiding behavior, 22, 35, 102
Home range, 109-110
Hunting behavior, 114-116
Hyla crucifer. See Spring peeper

I

Infections, 106
Injuries, recovery from, 105

Interference with nature, 111-112, 139-140
Iridoprocne bicolor. See Tree swallows
Iris versicolor. See Blue-flag iris

J

Juncus canadensis. See Canada rush

K

Killdeer, *73, 78*

L

Leatherleaf, *5*
Longevity
 of sperm cells, 56
 of turtles, 48-49, 51

M

Mammalian hibernation, 154
Map of the Digs, *14-15*
Map turtle
 gender differences, 50-51
 sexual maturity, 51
Marine turtles, 27
Marsh hawk, *154*
Mating, 42-61
 eastern box turtles, 51
 musk turtles, *57*
 spotted turtles, 61, *61*
 time of year, 55

Canada rush, *Juncus canadensis.*

Mayflies, *59*
  larvae, 32
Mayflowers, *45*
Meiolania turtles, 26
Melospiza melodia. See Song sparrow
Mermaid weed, *143*
Metabolism, 35
Mid-Cretaceous period, 26
Migration, 110-111
  spotted turtle, 121-125, 159-161
"Modern" turtle, 26
Musk turtle
  basking, 35-36
  courtship, 57
  mating, *57*
  nesting site, 136
  nonpulmonary respiration, 155
  subspecies variation in sexual
    maturity, 51

N

Nest, 66-67, *69,* 134
  hole, 66
  overwintering in, 136-137
  predators, 70-71
  snapping turtle, *86, 89*
    exit hole, *133*
    opening of, 131-134
  spotted turtle, 80-81
  visual concealment of, 81
Nesting, 56, 62-97
  environment, 72-73
  fields, map, 14-15
  observations, 65
  sites, 18, 73
    musk turtle, 136

  painted turtle, 136
  snapping turtle, 87-90, *88*
  spotted turtle, 93-97, *95*
  times, 75
Niobara Sea, 26
Nonpulmonary respiration, 155
Nuphar variegatum. See Yellow
  waterlily
Nycticorax nycticorax. See Black-
  crowned night heron
Nymphaea odorata. See White
  waterlily

O

Ornate box turtle, courtship
  behavior, 56-57
Osmunda cinnamomea. See Cinnamon
  fern
Osmunda regalis. See Royal fern
Overland migration, 110-111
  spotted turtle, 121-125, 159-161
Overwintering in nest, 136-137, 156
Oxygen deprivation during hiberna-
  tion, effects of, 21

P

Painted turtle, 65
  basking, 36
  courtship, 57-58
  eggs, 90
  freeze tolerance, 156
  gender differences, 50
  hatchling, 127, 134-135
  hibernation sites, 155

  home range, 109-110
  hunting, 83
  longevity of, 51
  nest, *69*
  nesting site, 73, 136
  nesting time, 75
  nonpulmonary respiration, 155
  pipping, *136*
  sexual maturity, 51
Paralysis at emergence, 21
Phalaris arundinacea. See Reedgrass
Philohela minor. See American
  woodcock
Pickerelweed, *99*
Pipping, 134, *136*
Plastron
  growth rings on, 48
  pond turtle, *16*
  snapping turtle, 29
Pleurodira, 25
Pond turtle, scutes, *16*
Pondweed, *115, 163*
Pontederia cordata. See Pickerelweed
Potamogetan natans. See Floating-leaf
  pondweed
Potamogetan sp. See Pondweed
Predaceous diving beetle, 20, *20*
Predators, 96, 122
  nest, 70-71
Proganochelys, 25
Proserpinaca sp. See Mermaid weed
Pussy willow, *43*

Q

Quiscalus quiscula. See Grackles,
  common

R

Raccoons, 122, *123*
  tracks, *71*
Rana catesbeiana. See Bullfrog
Rattlesnake manna grass, *6*
Redbelly turtle, home range, 109-110
Red maple, *46*
Redwinged blackbird, *22*
Reedgrass, *9, 44*
  sprouting, *50*
Relocating turtles, 111-112
Rosa palustris. See Swamp rose
Rose hips, *149*
Royal fern, *67, 93*

S

Sagittaria latifolia. See Broad-leaved
  arrowhead
Salamanders, spotted, 37
  mating, *39*
Salix discolor. See Pussy willow
Scutes
  irregularly patterned, *80*
  pond-turtle shell, *16*
Sedge, *44, 145*
  meadow, *104*
  tussock, *67*
Sense of homing, 110
Senses
  homing, 110
  sight, 111, 136
  smell, 74-75
Sexual dimorphism, 50-51
Sexual maturity, 51

Shell. *See* Carapace; Plastron
Side-necked turtles, 25
Size, and sexual maturity, 51
Skunk, 70, 76, *95,* 96
Smell, sense of, 74-75
Snapping turtle, 22-24
  basking, 35, 100, *101*
  carapace, *113*
  courtship and mating period, 55
  defensive behavior, 27-31
  diet, 116
  eggs, 90
  eye, *24*
  feeding, 114-115
  fighting among males, 56
  gender development, 82
  gender differences, 50
  hatchling, 131-134, *142, 152*
  hibernation sites, 157
  home range, 110
  hunting, 119, 115-116
  nest, *89*
    exit hole, *133*
    opening of, 131-134
    raided, *86*
  nesting, 83, 87-89, *88*
    sites, 73
    time, 75
  sexual dimorphism, 50
  sexual maturity, 51
Softshell turtle, 26, 29-30
  basking, 36
  gender differences, 50
  home range, 109-110
  nonpulmonary respiration, 155
Solidago nemeralis. See Gray
  goldenrod
Song sparrow, *43*

Sparganium sp. See Bur-reed
Sperm viability over time, 137
Sphagnum moss, *124*
Sphagnum sp. See Sphagnum moss
Spotted salamanders, 37
  mating, *39*
Spotted turtle, 14, 16-17, *26,* 43-44,
  46-50, 59-61, *67, 96,* 105-108, 112
  abdominal scute with irregular pat-
    tern, *80*
  basking, 34-36, *38,* 102
  carapace pattern, *18*
  coloration, 50
  courtship, 49-50, 55, 56
  eggs, 90
  feeding behavior, 115
  fighting, 52-55, *53*
  gender differences, 50
  hatchling, 129, 137-139, *139*
  hibernation sites, 157
  home range, 110
  hunting, 41
  longevity of, 51
  mating, 55, 61, *61*
  midsummer activity, 119-120
  migration, 121-125, 159-161
  nest, 80-81
  nesting, 76-78, 78-80, 93-97, *95*
    sites, 73
    time, 75
  plastron, *16*
  sense of homing, 110
  sexual maturity, 51
Spring emergence of hatchlings, 137
Spring peeper, *31, 37*
Sternotherus odoratus. See Musk turtle
Stress of hibernation, 155
Subspecies variation in sexual

maturity, 51
Summer dormancy, 102
Swale, map, 14-15
Swamp milkweed, *107*
Swamp rose, *34, 102, 149*
Sweetfern, 74, *74*
Synchronous emergence, 135

T

Terrapene c. carolina. See Eastern box
  turtle
Tortoises, feeding behavior, 115
Tree swallows, *54*
Triassic period, 25-26
Trionyx s. spinifera. See Eastern spiny
  softshell
Turtle
  age, determining, 48
  eggs, 90, 134
  embryonic development, 81-82, 85,
  112
  evolution, 24-27
  extinct species, 26-27
  feeding behavior, 115

fertilization in, 50, 137
"hidden-necked," 25
home range, 109
longevity of, 48-49
Meiolania, 26
"modern," 26
relocating, 111-112
sense of homing, 110
sexual maturity, 51
side-necked, 25
sperm viability over time, 137
vision, 111, 136
See also specific breeds
Tussock sedge, *67*

U

Underwater submersion, length of
  time, 22

V

Vaccinium macrocarpon. See
Cranberry

Vision, 111, 136

W

Weather
  and egg development, 81-82
  and gender differences, 82
White waterlily, *91*
Wood frogs, 37
Wood turtle, *157*
  basking, 36
  courtship behavior, 56
  eggs, 90
  gender differences, 50
  hibernation sites, 157
  nest, 84
  sense of homing, 110
  tracks in sand, *85*

Y

Yellow waterlily, *127*

ABOUT THE AUTHOR

David Carroll's passion for turtles began 40 years ago when, at age 8, he caught one of these creatures for the first time. Since then, he has continued to study the world of freshwater turtles, carefully recording details with pen as well as paint.

An artist by training, Mr. Carroll has taught in high schools and in diverse special needs programs and has produced work for the USDA Forest Service and for several publishers—*Harrowsmith Country Life, Reader's Digest, Country Journal,* Harcourt Brace Jovanovich, and Houghton Mifflin among them. His work has been exhibited in museums and galleries across the country, including Dartmouth College, the De Cordova Museum, and Hunt Institute for Botanical Documentation.

Mr. Carroll and his wife, Laurette, also an artist, live in Warner, New Hampshire. They have three grown children.